sound worship

a guide to making musical choices in a noisy world

scott aniol

REL CTIONS

www.religiousaffections.org

Sound Worship: A Guide to Making Musical Choices in a Noisy World

Copyright © 2010 by Scott Aniol

Published by Religious Affections Ministries
www.religiousaffections.org

First printing, 2010

Printed in the Unites States of America

ISBN-13 978-0-9824582-0-4
ISBN-10 0-9824582-0-7

Table of Contents

Introduction

MUSIC IS EVERYWHERE. It's in your car. It's in your home. It's on your TV. It's on your iPod. It's at the mall. It's at the restaurant. It's at amusement parks, parties, fairs, family reunions, and barbecues.

And music is at church.

You have choices. Never before in the history of mankind have there been so many music choices. With relative ease you can choose where to listen to music, when to listen to music, how long to listen to music, what artist to listen to, what style to listen to, what song to listen to, and how many times to listen to it.

What you can't choose is to *not* choose.

This is a book about making musical choices. But not just any choices. This is a book about making musical choices that are deliberately informed by the Word of God. It is about making choices that are discerning, wise, beneficial, and edifying.

This book is about making musical choices that will bring glory to God.

We live in a day of relativism, individualism, and pragmatism. Each of these vices presents significant challenges for making God-pleasing musical choices. Relativ-

1

ism teaches us that there is no right or wrong music. Individualism teaches us that we can choose whatever we happen to like. And pragmatism influences our theology of the church and convinces us to cater to the music preferences of the masses in order to draw them to our services. (End justifies means.)

Making musical choices in our society is no easy task, but it is a task we must face well-informed and well-equipped.

As a former pastor, music director, and now the director of a ministry that seeks to help equip and inform believers for this task, I have a strong burden that we think biblically about these issues. In January of 2009, BMH Books released my first book, *Worship in Song: a Biblical Approach to Music and Worship.* In that book I present a biblical, thoughtful, well-researched exploration of theological and philosophical ideas that can help believers understand music and worship.

Worship in Song specifically targets pastors and other Christians who really want to understand the foundational issues influencing worship and music philosophy. This means that the book is a somewhat in-depth presentation intended especially for those who have at least some theological or musical education.

Sound Worship, on the other hand, was written specifically for the average Christian who wants to learn how to make God-pleasing musical choices. I have taken what I consider to be the most important questions behind today's debates and sought to answer them in a brief, engaging, clear way. You won't find many technical details in this book unless they are absolutely necessary. I have tried to explain and illustrate important points with examples with which you can readily identify. If you want to understand the research and technical explanations of any of the points in this book, pick up a copy of *Worship in Song*. This book is intended to give you a starting place.

My prayer is that this book will help you wade through all of the myriads of musical choices you have for life and corporate worship. My hope is that you will gain what you need to make musical choices that truly glorify God.

Scott Aniol
September 2009
Simpsonville, SC
www.soundworshipbook.com

chapter one

Does Music Matter?

DOES MUSIC MATTER TO GOD? Should it matter to us?

We are living in a day when people — even Christians — see music as unimportant. Enjoyable, yes; but necessary or important? No.

We see this kind of thinking all around us. Music education is now considered extracurricular in schools. It's extra. It's not important. Support for the arts is waning in communities. Whereas families once viewed music as the highlight of the home, most families today have no interest.

This kind of thinking has, of course, influenced the church as well. What we believe theologically is important. How we live is important. But music? It's just something extra God has given us merely for enjoyment.

This certainly has ramifications for worship. If music is merely for enjoyment and is unimportant, then it really doesn't matter what kind of music we use in worship. God just doesn't really care.

Or does he?

In this chapter I would like to demonstrate that music

does indeed matter. It matters to God, and it should matter to us.

Music Matters Scripturally

If we want to discern whether music matters to God, we must first examine the Scriptures. What does the Bible have to say about music?

The Bible refers explicitly to music around 1,200 times. That in and of itself is not necessarily significant. The Bible refers to plants around 1,000 times, as well! But when we consider the kinds of things that are linked with music in the Bible or the contexts in which we find music in the Bible, it is clear that music matters.

Music in Worship

First, in the Bible music is highlighted as an important part of worship, both Old Testament Temple worship and New Testament Church worship.

In the Old Testament we find record of much of what went on in Jewish society. Israel was a theocracy, so its religious, civil, and social activities were all intertwined. Much of what went on in its society was related to its relationship with Yahweh but wasn't necessarily set apart specifically for corporate worship. This is certainly true of some of the music we have recorded for us in the Old Testament. Music is used for all sorts of purposes in the Bible: there are work songs,[1] war songs,[2] love songs,[3] songs for entertainment,[4] and songs of derision, mourning, and lamentation.[5] Since religion and society were intertwined in Jewish culture, the Old Testament relates many common uses of music in everyday life.

But some things were set apart specifically for corporate worship in the Temple. Before David's death, God allowed him to organize the Temple worship that would come to fulfillment under Solomon. We find this organization in 1 Chronicles 22 and following. Only the Levites *High Priests* were permitted to do work in the Temple, and at that time there were 38,000 men 30 years old and older. David divided these men for specific tasks: 24,000 were to be in charge of the work in the Temple, 6,000 were to be officers and judges, 4,000 were to be gatekeepers, and "4,000 shall offer praises to the LORD with the instruments that I have made for praise" (1 Chronicles 23:5).

We find two things of interest in this. First, it is significant that only Levites were allowed to perform music in the Temple. Only those who were specifically chosen and trained could serve in this capacity. Second, it is also noteworthy that God specifically says that he had designed music for his praise.

David then gives these groups of men specific instructions about how they are to go about leading worship in the Temple, and in chapter 25 he specifically addresses the musicians.

It is quite significant that David took so much time, under direction from the Lord, to set apart these Levites for the purpose of making music in the Temple. Furthermore, it is interesting to note how connected this music is with prophesy — direct revelation from God (1 Chronicles 25:1).

So in the organization of the Temple worship in the Old Testament, God ordained that there be priests and leaders and gatekeepers and musicians, and these musicians were specifically involved in leading the corporately gathered people in praise of God. God set apart music as one of the things he deemed important for his worship. He didn't set apart farmers or shepherds or builders; he did set apart musicians. We see this clearly in the instructions for Temple worship and in the Psalms, as well.

This is reflected also in New Testament Church worship:

> Addressing one another in psalms and hymns and spiritual songs, singing and making melody to the

Lord with all your heart (Ephesians 5:19).

Here, in the epistle most directly focused on the Church, we find a command to include music in our church worship. The parallel passage in Colossians 3:16—17 makes this congregational emphasis even more clear with its discussions in this context of the church as one body. The terms used here signify both vocal and instrumental music — "singing" being a translation of a term to signify vocal singing, and "making melody" a translation of a term meaning to play on a stringed instrument.

So in both the Old Testament and in the New Testament, music (both vocal and instrumental) is directly connected to and even commanded for corporate worship, along with preaching, praying, giving, etc. We'll look more later at why God set apart music for congregational worship, but for now it's at least instructive that he did.

This in itself should signify the importance and significance of music.

Music and Truth

Second, in the Bible music is highlighted as an important vehicle to communicate God's truth.

The parallel passage to Ephesians 5:19 addresses a second Scriptural purpose for music that is found throughout the pages of the Bible.

> Let the word of Christ dwell in you richly, teaching and admonishing one another in all wisdom, singing psalms and hymns and spiritual songs, with thankfulness in your hearts to God (Colossians 3:16).

Paul commands the Church at Colossi to let the Word of Christ dwell in them, music being an important accompanying vehicle. I'll explain in Chapter 3 why I don't believe that teaching propositional truth is all that is in view in this verse, but that is certainly part of the power of music — it can accompany and enhance God's truth.

Songs throughout the Bible are filled with God's truth. Just survey the Jewish hymnal — the Psalms — and you will find enough theology to fill a systematic theology. God could have presented that truth in any number of ways, but he chose to do so with art — poetry set to an appropriate tune. *It indicates the importance God puts on beaut*

We can find many examples of this in the New Testament, as well. There are many passages in the Epistles that scholars agree were written in a distinctly poetic form and likely set to music and sung in the early church. Examples include Philippians 2:6—11, 1 Timothy 3:16, 2 Timothy 2:11—13, John 1:1-18, Ephesians 1:1—11, 2:14—16, Colossians 1:15—20, and Hebrews 1:3.

Sacred songs are important vehicles for the communication of God's truth to his people.

Music and Emotion

Third, in the Bible music is highlighted as an important tool to sanctify our emotions.

In 1 Samuel 16:23 David uses music to soothe Saul's uneasy emotional state. We see the same kind of thing happening in Acts 16:25 when Paul and Silas were in prison. Instead of letting fear and depression overcome their spirits, they sang hymns. James 5:13 also talks about the emotional benefit of singing — it helps us express cheer.

We'll talk about this more in Chapter 3, but the Bible highlights music's ability to express and change emotion. This is the primary thrust of Colossians 3:16. The "teaching" that occurs through music is more than just teaching propositional truth to the mind. That can't be the only thing in view here because there are other better means to teach the mind than with music, and the parallel passage, Ephesians 5:19, talks about pure instrumental music. Music by itself doesn't teach the mind; music teaches the emotions. I'll elaborate more on this point in Chapter 3.

Music and Beauty

Fourth, in the Bible music is highlighted as an important means for expressing beauty, thus leading us to know Supreme Beauty.

The glory of God is one of those sometimes nebulous concepts that we don't often really get our minds around. But when we look at the kind of language that is used in Scripture to describe God's glory, it is clear that the idea that most closely connects with glory is the idea of beauty. The Bible is filled with aesthetic terminology to describe God. God's glory is his beauty, and his beauty is magnified when his people delight in lesser forms of beauty. In the Bible, beautiful music is often used as a way to magnify and praise the beauty of God himself.

Psalm 19:1 and Romans 1:20 both tell us how the beauty of creation displays the beauty of God and points man to him. Music as an expression of God-like beauty can do the same. We'll discuss the importance of beauty more fully in Chapter 5.

This is why music matters! It is not incidental or unimportant. It is not something neutral merely for our entertainment. Scripture is clear that music is significant for the Christian life and the glory of God. Music matters. Throughout the remaining chapters of this book, I will address and explain further the significance of each of these Scriptural emphases.

Still some might insist that music doesn't matter. That it's unimportant. If you're still skeptical, I leave you with some testimonies from church history.

Music develops the mind.

Music Matters Historically

Basil of Caesarea (330—379)

"A psalm is the tranquility of souls, the arbitrator of peace, restraining the disorder and turbulence of thoughts, for it softens the passion of the soul and moderates its unruliness. A psalm forms friendships, unites the divided, mediates between enemies. For who can still consider him an enemy with whom he has sent forth on voice to God? So that the singing of psalms brings love, the greatest of good things, contriving harmony like some bond of union and uniting the people in the symphony of a single choir.

"A psalm drives away demons, summons the help of angels, furnishes arms against nightly terrors, and gives respite from daily toil; to little children it is safety, to men in their prime an adornment, to the old a solace, to women their most fitting ornament. It peoples the solitudes, it brings agreement to market places. To novices it is a beginning; to those who are advancing, an increase; to those who are concluding, a confirmation. A psalm is the voice of the Church. It gladdens feast days, it creates grief which is in accord with God's will, for a psalm brings a tear even from a heart of stone."[6]

Ambrose (c. 340—397)

"A psalm is the blessing of the people, the praise of God . . . the joy of liberty, the noise of good cheer, and the echo of gladness. It softens anger, it gives release from anxiety, it alleviates sorrow; it is protection at night, instruction by day, a shield in time of fear, a feast of holiness, the image of tranquility, a pledge of peace and harmony, which produces one song from various and sundry voices in the manner of a stringed instrument. The day's dawning resounds with a psalm, with a psalm its passing echoes."[7]

John Chrysostom (c. 347—407)

"God established the psalms, in order that singing might be both a pleasure and a help. From strange chants harm, ruin, and many grievous matters are brought in, for those things that are lascivious and vicious in all songs settle in parts of the mind, making it softer and weaker; from spiritual psalms, however, proceeds much of value, much utility, much sanctity."[8]

Augustine (354—430)

"The sound of jubilation signifies that love, born in our heart, that cannot be spoken. And to whom is such jubilation due if not to God; for he is the ineffable One, he Whom no words can define. But if you cannot speak him into words, and yet you cannot remain silent, what else is left to you if not the song of jubilation, the rejoicing of your heart beyond all words, the immense latitude of the joy without limit of syllables."[9]

Martin Luther (1483—1546)

"We have put this music to the living and holy Word of God in order to sing, praise and honor it. We want the beautiful art of music to be properly used to serve her dear Creator and his Christians. He is thereby praised and honored and we are bade better and stronger in faith when his holy Word is impressed on our hearts by sweet music."[10]

John Calvin (1509—1564)

Just because one is wrong in an area doesn't mean one is wrong in every one.

"And in truth we know by experience that singing has great force and vigor to move and inflame the hearts of men to invoke and praise God with a more vehement and ardent zeal. Care must always be taken that the song be neither light nor frivolous; but that it have weight and majesty (as Augustine says), and also, there is a great difference between music which one makes to entertain men at table and in their houses, and the Psalms which are sung in the Church in the presence of God and his angels.

God is transcendent.

Now among the other things which are proper for re-creating man and giving him pleasure, music is either the first, or one of the principal; and it is necessary for us to think that it is a gift of God deputed for that use. Moreover, because of this, we ought to be the more careful not to abuse it, for fear of soiling and contaminating it, converting it to our condemnation, where it was dedicated to our profit and use. If there were no other consideration than this alone, it ought indeed to move us to moderate the use of music, to make it serve all honest things; and that it should not give occasion for our giving free rein to dissolution, or making ourselves effeminate in disordered delights, and that it should not become the instrument of lasciviousness nor of any shamelessness."[11]

Jonathan Edwards (1703—1758)

"The best, most beautiful, and most perfect way that we have of expressing a sweet concord of mind to each other is by music."[12]

Music communicates.

Conclusion

Does music matter?

Does it matter to God? Should it matter to us?

In my opinion, the evidence is overwhelming. The Bible's hundreds of references to music and its power and benefits, music's ability to give us expression for our affection to God and teach us what we should be feeling about God, a theological understanding of the beauty and glory of God being reflected in beautiful music, and the testimony after testimony of Christian leaders throughout history all attest to the fact that music matters.

Why, all of a sudden, in the 20th and 21st centuries do we insist that it doesn't matter?

I'm not at this point making any points about specific music styles or cultures. All I'm arguing is that music is important, and we should take the time to make careful and informed decisions about the music we allow into our lives and worship.

The goal of this book is to help you make those kinds

of informed decisions. Through the rest of this book, we will discuss each of the issues expressed in this chapter to help us understand the importance of music for life and worship.

chapter two

Is the Bible Enough?

"Caleb is not the boss."

One of the most challenging concepts for young children to learn is that they are not the ultimate authority over their lives! Each of us is born believing ourselves to be the center of the universe. My wife and I are currently trying to help our two-year-old son learn the truth that he is not the authority by having him repeat on occasion the phrase, "Caleb is not the boss."

But this problem, as you know, does not end with childhood. We each struggle with authority all of our lives! Especially when it comes to ethical decisions, we struggle with who has the authority to tell us what to do.

When it comes to making musical choices, we find ourselves asking, "Who has the authority to tell us what music we may or may not listen to?"

For Christians, our clear answer is that God is our authority, and the Bible is our sufficient source of that authority.

But even having settled that question, a few others still linger as we make decisions about music:

1. Does the Bible even say anything about musical

style?

2. Is there even such a thing as music that doesn't please the Lord?

3. Is the Bible all we need to make God-pleasing decisions?

The Bible Is Sufficient

Ultimately, the place we must go when asking questions of how to please the Lord is the Bible. One of the hallmark doctrines of Protestant churches is the doctrine of the sufficiency of Scripture. But what, exactly, does the sufficiency of Scripture mean?

Probably one of the clearest passages that articulates this doctrine is found in 2 Timothy 3:

> [14]But as for you, continue in what you have learned and have firmly believed, knowing from whom you learned it [15]and how from childhood you have been acquainted with the sacred writings, which are able to make you wise for salvation through faith in Christ Jesus. [16]All Scripture is breathed out by God and profitable for teaching, for reproof, for correction, and for training in righteousness, [17]that the man of God may be competent, equipped for every good work.

The Bible is Sufficient for Salvation

The first point we can draw from this text is that the Bible is sufficient to give us the teaching we need for salvation. Paul tells Timothy in verse 15 that the "sacred writings," a phrase used often to refer to the Scriptures, are sufficient ("able") to give him the truth he needs ("to make you wise") for salvation.

The Holy Spirit uses the Word of God in a person's life as the means through which that person comes to faith in Christ. The Holy Spirit is certainly the agent of regeneration, but he does not somehow miraculously "zap" an individual without that person understanding the truths of the gospel. Regeneration is supernatural, but it is accomplished through the proclamation of God's Word.

For example, Paul says in Romans 10 that people will not come to salvation without someone preaching the Word of God to them (v. 14) because "faith comes from hearing, and hearing through the word of Christ" (v. 17). In Luke 10, a lawyer asks Jesus, "What shall I do to inherit eternal life" (v. 25)? Jesus replies, knowing the lawyer was testing him, "What is written in the Law" (v. 26)? In other words, everything you need for eternal life is found within the Scriptures. In Luke 16, when the rich man, in Hades, asks Abraham to send Lazarus to his father's house to warn his brothers about judgement (vv. 27—28), Abraham replies, "They have Moses and the Prophets; let them hear them" (v. 29). In other words, all the warning necessary to lead a person to salvation is found within the Word of God.

So the Bible is all anyone needs to lead him to faith in Jesus Christ. But that is not the only thing for which the Bible is sufficient according to 2 Timothy 3.

The Bible is Sufficient for Sanctification

Not only is the Bible all anyone needs for salvation, but the Bible also is sufficient to makes us "competent, equipped for every good work" (2 Timothy 3:17). The word translated "competent" and the word translated "equipped" are actually different forms of the same term that communicate the idea of being perfectly adapted for a task.

What an incredible truth! The Bible equips us to do absolutely everything that God expects us to do. But upon what basis can Paul make this statement? Let's look back up in verse 16 for explanation.

The first statement about Scripture that Paul articulates is that it is inspired, literally "breathed out by God." In Jeremiah 1:9, God told Jeremiah, "Behold, I have put my words in your mouth." This is the idea communicated by the Greek term *Theopneustos* in 2 Timothy 3:16. *Theos* is the Greek term for "God" and *neuma* means "breath." So God literally breathed out the very words of Scripture. He did not dictate the Bible as if the human authors were mere secretaries, but as 2 Peter 1:21 tells us, "Men spoke from God as they were carried along by the Holy Spirit." Each human author wrote of his own volition in his own writing style, but because he was carried along by the Holy Spirit as he wrote, we can be confident that every word in the Bible has been breathed out by God himself.

We draw several important implications from this truth that every word of the Bible was inspired by God. First, because the Bible came from God, and God is both true and unchanging, the Bible is therefore both inerrant (without error) and infallible (incapable of error). In Matthew 5:18 Jesus said that not one word of Scripture will pass away until it is all fulfilled. In John 10:35 he said that "Scripture cannot be broken." The Word of God is perfect.

But also, the fact that the Bible was breathed out by God implies its authority. No Christian would deny that God is the ultimate authority. Therefore it follows that if God is our authority, then his infallible Word is likewise our authority.

The Bible is sufficient to perfectly equip us for every good work because it is from God himself. We can be certain that we have everything we need in the Bible itself in order to please God because it is from him. It is perfect, it is complete, and it is authoritative.

But the Bible is not only authoritative, it is also profitable, as 2 Timothy 3:16 tells us. And remember, the beginning of the verse identified "*all* Scripture." Every part of the Word of God has profitability for the Christian.

The profitability of Scripture further undergirds its sufficiency for us. The Bible is our authority, and every part of it is profitable. The term translated "profitable" is a word that means beneficial, productive, and sufficient. Inherent in this word itself is the sufficiency of Scripture, articulated so well in Jude 3 where the author says that the Scripture was "*once* delivered for all the saints." We should expect no additional revelation from God. The Bible is sufficient to equip us.

The Bible is sufficient for both our doctrinal needs and our practical needs. The terms "teaching" and "reproof" are most naturally connected to instructing and correcting in areas of doctrine, and the terms "correction" and "training in righteousness" carry the idea of adjusting and nurturing right conduct.

The Bible is sufficient, then, as our authority and guide. It thoroughly equips us to believe and live in a way that brings ultimate glory to God.

What the Sufficiency of Scripture Does Not Mean

We have seen, then, from 2 Timothy 3, that the Bible is sufficient for our salvation and our sanctification. Because it came directly from the breath of God, it is sufficient as our authority and as our profitable guide.

However, this understanding does not end all debate as to what, exactly, this sufficiency really means. For example, if we were to discuss how the sufficiency of Scripture applies to making musical choices in our lives, some would argue that since the Bible doesn't really talk at all about musical style, then style must be unimportant to God. If the Bible is sufficient, and if the Bible doesn't address a particular issue, then we don't need to worry about it, right?

The debate really centers on what, exactly, the phrase "perfectly equipped to every good work" means. The phrase could be taken one of two ways. Let me illustrate the two possible meanings of "perfectly equipped."

After I graduated from college, I lived a year as a bachelor. I entered pastoral ministry in Illinois two days after my graduation, proposed to Becky a week later, but had to wait a year for her to graduate before we married.

I lived for that year by myself in a small apartment, and for a graduation present, Becky gave me a cookbook called, *Help! My Apartment Has a Kitchen!* She wanted me to eat healthy meals during the year I was alone and knew I wouldn't do it unless the recipes were very simple and detailed. (She had already discovered my affinity for Burger King.) In a sense, she gave me the cookbook and said, "This cookbook will perfectly equip you to make healthy meals for yourself. Use it!"

It wasn't long before I recognized, however, that even though the cookbook gave me very clear instructions about how to make meals, I needed more information than just what was in the book to help me. I found myself calling Becky from the grocery store asking her where to find certain ingredients and repeatedly calling her while I cooked because I needed help interpreting various phrases, terms, and instructions.

Now, there wasn't really anything deficient in the cookbook itself. It really was all I needed to make healthy, pleasing meals. The deficiency was in myself. I needed other information, such as where to find things in the grocery store, the definition of terms, and how to perform certain actions the cookbook took for granted in order to cook the meal. The cookbook was a guide, but I needed more information to apply its instructions.

That's one way of interpreting "perfectly equipped." But here's another way.

Imagine that my wife leaves me at home with our two children while she goes to an overnight ladies' retreat. As part of her preparation for leaving, she provides me with a list of things that I should do while she's gone — feed the kids certain meals, bathe them, put them to bed at a certain time, make sure to pick up after them, etc. She tells me, "This list will perfectly equip you to care for the children while I am away."

Because of the care she has put into the list, I can be certain that if I accomplish all of the instructions on the list, I won't have to worry about anything else. If a decision arises that she has not addressed on the list, I can safely assume that she really doesn't care what decision I make. For example, the list says nothing about which pajamas to put on my son before bed, so I can make that decision on my own.

In other words, if I stick to the list, I know I'll do everything correctly. Anything not on the list really doesn't matter.

People approach biblical application in one of these two ways. For some people, the Bible is like a list. God gave us a list of things that he wanted us to do, and a list of things he wanted us to avoid, and so if something is not on the list, God doesn't care about it.

For these people, music would be one of those issues that God doesn't care about because musical style is not on "the list."

Others, however, view the Bible more like the cookbook. It has everything we need to please God within itself, but sometimes we'll need some other information to apply its instructions.

So which way is correct?

The best way to discover how we should view Scripture is to observe statements from Scripture itself. First, consider Galatians 5:19—21:

> Now the works of the flesh are evident: sexual immorality, impurity, sensuality, [20]idolatry, sorcery, enmity, strife, jealousy, fits of anger, rivalries, dissensions, divisions, [21]envy, drunkenness, orgies, and things like these.

Here we have a list of sinful actions that we should avoid, things like sexual immorality, jealousy, and drunkenness. The fact that this is a list may suggest that the

"Bible-as-list" view is the correct one, but notice that Paul does not intend for this to be an exhaustive list. Notice that he ends the list with, "and things like these." In other words, this list, like others throughout Scripture, is meant to be merely a representative list. God expects us to read lists like this and consider other actions that we should also avoid because they are "like" the things on the list. The fact that Paul called these works "evident" indicates that we should be able to discern them.

Consider also, Hebrews 5:14:

> But solid food is for the mature, for those who have their powers of discernment trained by constant practice to distinguish good from evil.

The author of Hebrews says that a mark of spiritual maturity is having your powers of discernment trained so that you can distinguish between good and evil even if you don't have specific instructions about a particular issue. Someone who is immature needs specific instructions.

We who are parents understand this well. Before my two-year-old son goes to bed each evening, I tell him to clean up his toys. Often, I have to give him additional, very specific instruction. "Pick up that blue car. Put it in the box. Pick up that *Curious George* book. Put it on the shelf."

But every so often, I tell Caleb to clean up his toys, and that's all the instruction he needs. Without me giving him specific instructions, he discerns that he needs to put all of his books away, box up his Legos, and put away his toy cars. It is at those moments that I recognize the beginnings of maturity.

The same is true for Christians. The Bible is not a list of commands and prohibitions. It is not an encyclopedia of specific instructions for how to please God.

Instead, the Bible is an all-sufficient guide for developing a God-pleasing worldview. It doesn't give us specific lists that cover all possible situations we may encounter in our lives. It gives us ways to order our thinking so that we will choose what is right even when God has not explicitly told us what to do in a given situation. There are hundreds of situations we face today that the Bible doesn't specifically address because we encounter issues that the original authors and audiences would have never imagined. The Bible does not perfectly equip us for every good work by telling us the exact right decisions to make for every situation we may face.

Rather, the Bible provides us with hundreds of narratives illustrating specific situations that may resemble the ones we'll face. It gives us thousands of commands and prohibitions from which we may draw principles to apply to new issues. It presents us with a display of the nature and character of God so that we may make exactly the kinds of decisions he would make without him having to tell us. Actually, those who insist that if the Bible doesn't address something then it doesn't matter what we do are limiting the profitability of Scripture. The Bible applies to everything!

A few years ago I remodeled our home's walk-up attic and turned it into a master suite. Sometimes when particular questions arose I asked for my wife's opinion to make sure I would choose something that would please her. But often, because I had grown to understand her desires and preferences, I was able to make decisions I knew would please her without even asking. This is what the Bible enables us to do as we seek to please our God.

So the sufficiency of Scripture does not mean that the Bible is all we need to please the Lord. It does mean that the Bible is the only perfect, authoritative revelation we need. But we will often require additional information in order to apply the Bible's principle to life.

For example, in order to please the Lord with my driving, I need to know the rules of the road, what the speed limit is, and the mechanics of driving. In order to please the Lord with my body, I need to understand something of the nature of nutrition, healthy exercising, and the effect of certain substances (like nicotine or caffeine) on the body.

And in order to make musical choices that please the Lord, I need to understand something of how music communicates and affects spirituality.

The Bible does not explicitly tell us what kind of music pleases the Lord or what kind of music does not or even if such categories exist. The Bible does not explicitly tell us how music works or how we relate to music. But this does not mean that our musical choices are left to mere whim or preference. Just like with many other issues, we may draw certain implications from biblical statements about music and examples of music, and we may look to extra-biblical informational authorities to gain necessary understanding of music so that we may apply the Bible's clear principles to it. We must "test everything" and "hold fast what is good" (1 Thessalonians 5:21).

Training in Application

This kind of application of the Scripture, as Hebrews

5:19 states, is going to take diligent work and training. Paul tell us in 1 Timothy 4:7, "Train yourself for godliness." Literally, "Continually train yourself to be godly." We may say that we want to please the Lord; we may say that we want to make right choices in our lives; but we are often unwilling to work hard and train ourselves to be godly. Skillful application of the Bible comes only from disciplined training.

Sometimes we assume that godliness is something that occurs naturally for the Christian. We think that Christians will make right choices automatically and that biblical application will be easy. However, 1 Timothy 6:11 teaches that believers must actively pursue godliness: "But you, man of God, flee from all this, and pursue righteousness, godliness, faith, love, endurance and gentleness."

The process of sanctification, while inevitable, is not automatic. The Bible teaches that believers will surely persevere, but it also teaches that perseverance is an active process for the believer. Christians must actively pursue godliness. It requires training. This word, "train," in 1 Timothy 4:7 is in the present tense, which emphasizes that this is an ongoing, continual process. It is a translation of a Greek term from which we get our English words "gymnasium" and "gymnastics." It speaks of rigorous, strenuous, self-sacrificing training. Paul compares training for godliness to the physical training of an athlete.

Paul's emphasis is this: strive after godliness. Pursue it. It is not an option. Spiritual self-discipline has eternal value and is the key to godly living. Learning to rightly apply the Bible to life's situations is something that takes effort, discipline, endurance, and patience.

As we seek to apply the Bible to contemporary issues, we must contextualize scriptural principles to modern issues, and this is a two-step process. First, we must read the Bible as the original audience would have read it and extract timeless principles. This step requires understanding of the original readers' contexts and prior understanding of various issues, and sometimes this may require consultation of extra-biblical sources including language tools, dictionaries, histories, and archeological studies.

Second, we apply those timeless principles to contemporary issues. This step requires understanding the nature of the contemporary issue, and again, this may require the consultation of extra-biblical sources. Students of the Bible use extra-biblical sources of truth regularly as they *interpret* the Bible. Why, then, do some refuse to use extra-biblical sources as they *apply* the Bible?

As we consult extra-biblical sources in both of these steps, we recognize that our ultimate source of authority is the Word of God, which authorizes all of our knowledge. But we also recognize that the Bible itself testifies to the real authority of general revelation as a source of truth (Romans 1:20). In other words, although the Bible is our supreme authority and source of truth, real truth exists outside its pages, and that truth informs our understanding as we approach the task of application.

Biblical application is sometimes hard work! The Christian life is not one of passive living. It should be one of active, hard-working, disciplined training toward godliness. God commands us to actively pursue godliness through intense training, which includes how to rightly apply the Bible to all of our choices.

So if our goal is to apply biblical principles to issues related to music, we must have at least a cursory understanding of how music works and how we relate to music. If you want to make good decisions in the Bible translation debate, you must understand something of translation philosophy and the history of Bible translation. If you want to make good decisions regarding whether a Christian today should consume alcohol as a beverage, you must understand the nature of alcohol and the cultural conditions of the Ancient Near East. The same is true for music. This does not mean that you must understand music theory or be a practicing musician. But you must have a basic understanding of the way the music communicates if you are going to apply the Bible's principles about communication to this medium.

Applying the Bible to Musical Choices

So as we enter a discussion of musical choices that please the Lord, we must acknowledge several important points.

First, the Bible is sufficient as our authority in these matters. We must immerse ourselves in the truths of Scripture to arrive at God-pleasing decisions about music.

Second, we need to give careful attention to other information that may be helpful in our decision making. In particular, we need to understand something about how music communicates. We need to understand the purposes of music in our lives in general and especially for worship. We need to understand the nature of beauty and its relationship to the glory of God.

Understanding some of these things may require careful thinking and work. But that is what is necessarily for

those who want to please God with their choices by apply-
ing the Bible to contemporary decisions, including what
music we will enjoy.

chapter three

Why Do We Sing In Church?

I ONCE KNEW A MAN who attended a church where he loved the preaching but hated the music. He told me that each Sunday he actually planned to arrive 45 minutes late to the service because by then the music would be finished and he could enjoy the message.

I know another man who refuses to sing during the services at his church because he doesn't like to sing. For him, singing hymns is just for those who enjoy it. He is willing to let other people do what they like to do, but he is just there for the preaching.

I know of other people who demand that their churches cater to their musical preferences. If their church won't play music that they like, they'll just look for another church. Or we all know of churches that have multiple services or even multiple campuses, each tailored to a particular style of music.

Each of these scenarios shares something in common, and it has to do with what the people involved view as the primary purpose of music in church. These people view music as either completely irrelevant or just as something to enjoy doing as they gather for worship. If we were to ask these people what they think the purpose of music in worship is, they'd probably answer something like this: sacred music is right truth packaged nicely. We take good, doctrinal truth, and we set it to something we enjoy so that it will be memorable and so that we can learn the truth. There is some validity to an answer like this, but I think such an answer is inadequate.

The reason this kind of answer is inadequate is that it completely misses the primary reason that we have sacred music. The people who answer this way focus only on the words of sacred music and give no consideration to the actual music itself or even to the poetic form of the words. The danger with that kind of view is that it leads to the philosophy that as long as the words are biblically sound, we can use whatever musical forms we enjoy, or we can eliminate music in worship altogether.

So why do we sing in worship?

In order to answer the question of why we use music in worship, we need to first answer the question, what is worship?

What is Worship?

The primary text that explains to us the essence of

worship is in John 4:21—24. In this passage Jesus meets the Samaritan woman at the well. In order to change the subject off of her sin, the woman asks Jesus about the proper outward forms of worship. The Samaritans say we need to worship on Mt. Gerazim, the Jews believe we must worship on Mt. Zion; so what is the proper way to worship? Jesus replies in verse 21:

> Woman, believe me, the hour is coming when neither on this mountain nor in Jerusalem will you worship the Father. [22]You worship what you do not know; we worship what we know, for salvation is from the Jews. [23]But the hour is coming, and is now here, when the true worshipers will worship the Father in spirit and truth, for the Father is seeking such people to worship him. [24]God is spirit, and those who worship him must worship in spirit and truth.

Both the Jews and the Samaritans were preoccupied with the outward forms of worship, and for good reason. God had established very specific forms for Jewish worship in the Old Testament. But Jesus replied that with his coming, the outward rituals were no longer necessary. Instead, he focused on what the essence of worship has always been — response of the spirit to truth. Worship happens when believers understand truth about God and respond rightly in their spirits.

In this way, worship really should encompass all of life for the Christian. Worship is not limited to corporate church gatherings on Sunday morning. In every moment of our lives we should be responding rightly with our spirits to truth about God. However, for the sake of our discussion here, let's focus our attention specifically on congregational worship and the music we choose for these gatherings.

Worship in Truth

The first essential component of worship is truth. This assertion has two implications.

First, we must worship according to God's instructions found in his Word. We cannot worship however we please; we must worship how God pleases. Notice what Christ says in verse 22: "You worship what you do not know; we worship what we know, for salvation is from the Jews." In other words, the Jews at that time were worshiping correctly because they were following the instructions about worship given to them in the Word of God. The Samaritans had invented their own ways of worshiping God.

So what is this true way to worship that God has commanded in his Word? First, we must worship only the one true and living God. This is expressed in the First Commandment: "You shall have no other gods before me" (Exodus 20:3).

Second, we must worship through the person of Jesus Christ. His sacrifice is what makes our worship possible, and it is only through his high priestly ministry that we may even approach the Holy God in worship.

> But when Christ appeared as a high priest of the good things that have come, then through the greater and more perfect tent (not made with hands, that is, not of this creation) [12]he entered once for all into the holy places, not by means of the blood of goats and calves but by means of his own blood, thus securing an eternal redemption. [13]For if the blood of goats and bulls, and the sprinkling of defiled persons with the ashes of a heifer, sanctify for the purification of the flesh, [14]how much more will the blood of Christ, who through the eternal Spirit offered himself without blemish to God, purify our conscience from dead works to serve the living God (Hebrews 9:11—14).

Third, God has given us clear prescriptions and examples of the elements we may include in our corporate New Testament worship. These God-approved elements are Scripture reading (1 Timothy 4:13), preaching (2 Timothy 4:2), singing (Ephesians 5:19, Colossians 3:16), prayer (1 Timothy 2:1), the ordinances of baptism and the Lord's Supper (Acts 2:41—42), and giving (2 Corinthians 16). If we are to worship in truth, we may not add any other elements based upon our own ingenuity or creativity.

So first, to worship in truth means that we worship according to how God has commanded in his Word.

Second, worship in truth means that the content of our worship must present truth from God. This means that preaching is certainly important as an element of corporate worship. This is why Paul commands Timothy to "give attention to the public reading of Scripture" (1 Timothy 4:13). And this *is* one of the reasons we sing in a church service. The texts of our hymns should contain rich truth about God. We cannot worship without understanding biblical truth.

Worship in Spirit

But worship does not end with simply understanding truth. As Christ says to the woman in John 4, God desires those who will worship him in *spirit* and truth. In the original text there is only one preposition, "in," that governs both nouns. In other words, it should read "in spirit and truth" not "in spirit and *in* truth" as some translations render the phrase. What this indicates is that these two qualities are not separate characteristics of true worship. They are essentially connected. Without one or the other there is no true worship.

Now what did Jesus mean when he referred to "spirit"? Consider the context. The woman was asking about specific locations; which mountain is correct, this one or that one? In his answer Christ was de-emphasizing the physical locations and rituals of worship in favor of immaterial, spiritual responses — that is, response of the heart; response of the affections.

True worship involves responding to truth with our hearts. Christ himself said that the greatest command-ment is to love the Lord with our whole being (Mark 12:30). Our affections are at the center of what it means to worship the Lord.

Now, we need to stop for just a moment and consider this notion of the affections, because it is often misunder-stood today. When I say "affections," I am not referring to merely physical feelings, things like butterflies in the stomach, goosebumps, tears, or exhilaration. Affection may be accompanied by physical feelings, but the feelings themselves do not define the affection.

There are three reasons we must separate the idea of spiritual affections from physical feelings in our under-standing. First, individual personality plays a significant part in what kind of feelings or the intensity of the feel-ings you may experience along with an affection. Some people are naturally extroverts. We might say about a person like this that "he wears his emotions on his sleeve." What we mean is that he is a naturally expressive person, and so the affections he has internally tend to reveal themselves quite readily in observable, physical ways. But we cannot define the affection by the feeling because someone else may not experience that same kind of external feeling.

Second, we may experience different kinds of feelings at different times even though we have the same affections. Sometimes, when I have the affection of joy, I feel peaceful, warm, comfortable, and serene. Other times when I have the affection we call "joy," I feel boisterous, energetic, and lively. Same affection, but much different ways of physically "feeling" that affection depending on circumstances.

But the primary reason we cannot equate spiritual affections with physical feelings is that physical feelings can be stimulated without any thought or spiritual affection whatsoever. You may have a physical feeling that accompanies the affection of joy, but that same kind of feeling can be artificially stimulated by riding a roller coaster.

The difference between feelings that are merely chemical responses to a stimulus and affections that result in feelings is like the difference between laughing because you've been tickled and laughing because you get a joke. When I tickle my son and he has certain feelings that result in laughing, nothing is going on in his mind intellectually. He is merely responding to a stimulus. However, if I were to tell you a joke, you would have the same physical response of laughing, but it would be because you have intellectually comprehended the punch line.

Let me give you another example. One night when I was in college, a friend of mine snuck into my bunk bed while I was out of the room just before "lights out" in the residence hall. I came into the room, turned off the lights, and got into my bed without ever noticing that he was there. After a few moments of silence, my friend shouted, "Boo!" and I dove out of the bed. I certainly experienced a feeling of exhilaration! But that feeling had nothing to do with an internal, spiritual response of my affections. It was merely a chemical response to an external stimulus.

When Jesus says worship in spirit, he is referring to a response of our hearts after we have understood and affirmed truth, and it may or may not be accompanied by physical feelings.

Facilitating Worship in Spirit and Truth

So how can we worship in spirit and truth in a corporate gathering? It is fairly easy to list the kinds of things that we use in a church service for the purpose of teaching truth. Teaching, preaching, reading the Scriptures, and the lyrics of our hymns all help to teach truth to our minds.

But what about worshiping in spirit? How can we respond with our spirits after truth has been presented in corporate worship? We can, of course, simply tell the Lord that we love him or that we rejoice in him, but really, words are inadequate to express our hearts, aren't they?

Those who are parents know what it is to have no words to express the joy at the birth of a child. Those who have lost loved ones know how limited mere words can be to express the accompanying grief. Words alone are inadequate to express our affections.

Not only that, but words are also inadequate in teaching us what affections we should be expressing to God. I can tell you to "Rejoice in the Lord," but what do I mean by "rejoice"? Do I mean some kind of rousing enthusiasm that I might experience at a sporting event? Do I mean a restful, warm peace that I might have when watching my children play?

I can tell you to "Love God," but what do I mean by "love"? Do I mean the kind of love I have for pizza? Do I mean the kind of love I have for my wife or children? Do I mean the kind of "love" a teenage girl might express toward a rock star? Each of those could be called "love."

You see, not all emotion is created equal, and mere words do not contain the nuances necessary to distinguish between *kinds* of joy or *kinds* of love.

So if I want to express joy to the Lord, but I'm not quite sure how to express the kind of reverent joy he deserves instead of a flippant kind of joy, I need something to help me distinguish between the two. If I want to express love to God, but I'm not certain how to express acceptable love to him instead of romantic love, I need something to help me distinguish between the two.

You see, we need something besides mere words to help us both express our affections to God and teach us the qualities of right affections.

The Language of Our Spirits

God has gifted us with music to help us with the "spirit" side of worship. After we have understood truth about God, music is a tool that God has given us both as a language for the expression of our affections to God and to teach us the kinds of affections we should be expressing to him.

Expressing our Spirits

We find this two-fold benefit of music in worship expressed in what are perhaps the two best known passages in the New Testament that speak about music. The first is Ephesians 5:19:

> Addressing one another in psalms and hymns and spiritual songs, singing and making melody to the Lord with your heart.

Notice that the last phrase identifies the heart as the primary focus of music. Music provides a means to express our affections to the Lord. This can be done with or without words. Notice that the verse says "singing" — that's a word to designate vocal music most likely with words, and "making melody" — that's a word that literally refers to playing on a stringed instrument — music without words. So literally, "sing and strum with your heart to the Lord."

As we saw earlier, words are unable to adequately express what we feel. Sacred music — that is, poetry and music — provides us with the language we are lacking in the expression of our affections. So in a church service as we contemplate truth and goodness, we use music to help us take the next step and respond with our affections. We believe in the holiness of God, but when we put that truth to a fitting tune, we can express how we feel about that truth. We believe that Jesus sacrificed for us on the cross, but when we put that truth to a fitting tune, we can better express how we feel about that truth when mere words wouldn't be sufficient.

Now, emotion for its own sake is not what we're after. Many contemporary churches have it right when they insist that expression of emotion is a critical part of the church's work. However, they often have a misunderstanding of emotion and end up focusing on emotion for its own sake apart from the necessary connection to biblical truth. I'm afraid that many churches that have excellent doctrine but are using pop music with that doctrine are doing so because they confuse the physical feelings with true, biblical responses of the spirit — true affections. They also fail to recognize that not all emotion is the same. Some kinds of emotional expressions are simply inappropriate for the worship of God.

Teaching our Spirits

So music helps us express right affection for truth when we cannot adequately put it into words, and second, music actually teaches our emotions. No passage better illustrates this point of music as a teacher of the emotions than Colossians 3:16:

> Let the word of Christ richly dwell within you, with all wisdom teaching and admonishing one another with psalms and hymns and spiritual songs, singing with thankfulness in your hearts to God (NASB).

Notice that it says that we should teach and admonish each other with music.[13] Now I do not doubt that the teaching here involves using the words to teach truth and goodness as well. But the primary part of man that is being taught by music is his emotions. This is evidenced by the phrase, "with thankfulness in your hearts," emphasizing the internal aspect. We saw the same internal, heart emphasis of music in Ephesians 5. Again, what these verses are talking about refers to more than just music with words; it refers to music without words as well. So music helps us actually teach believers' emotions.

We can see this kind of thing evidenced in Scripture. When Saul was in a terrible emotional state, David used music to change and mature his emotions (1 Samuel

16:23). When Paul and Silas were in prison, they used hymns to lift their spirits (Acts 16:25).

Just like we need teaching to correct our wrong thinking and our wrong acting, so we need teaching to correct our wrong feeling. And music is just that teacher. Our society today is filled with such wrong feelings. Accidentally cut someone off on the road and the rage rises right to the surface. But Christians have the same kinds of wrong feelings. And when we fill our lives with music that expresses rage, we are doing nothing to help our problem. We are not helping to sanctify our emotions.

I think one of the biggest problems in churches and especially with young people is an unbiblical, sentimental, sensual view of love. Again, this view of love is more about the feelings themselves than true, biblical affection. One of the factors that has led to this, I believe, is filling our lives with music that may not seem overtly evil, but it expresses a sentimental, smarmy, light, and fluffy view of life and love. And then, even worse, we bring the same kind of music into the church, and our view of love for God is equally wrong.

Instead, we must view all music, and sacred music in particular, as a tool to help us teach ourselves how we should be feeling — how we should be responding with our affections to truth.

Conclusion

So this is why we use music in church: First, we use music to help us express right affection to the Lord. When we understand truth, music helps us respond with our affections when we might not otherwise have the right words to say. Second, good music educates our emotions and tells us what we should be feeling. When we don't know what kind of affection we should have, or when we actually have the wrong kinds of emotions, good music can teach us what kind of affection is right.

We may draw several very important, practical applications from this understanding of the purpose of music in worship. First, setting the philosophy of music for a church falls under the responsibility of pastoral leadership just as setting the philosophy of preaching falls under pastoral authority. Expressions of the spirit and teaching the spirit are just as important and just as potentially dangerous as expressions of truth or teaching truth. This means that not just anyone in the church can demand a certain song or musical style no more than he can demand a certain doctrine. He can suggest or request, of course, but at the end of the day the final decisions must be left to pastoral authorities.

Second, active participation in the singing of the church is not optional. Since singing is not just pretty packaging for truth presentation but an essential, God-ordained means for the expression and teaching of right affections in worship, every worshiper must participate. We do not have a choice whether or not we sing any more than we have a choice whether or not to listen to preaching, participate in Scripture reading, live holy lives, or love God.

Third, only music that expresses emotions that are appropriate for worship should be used in worship. Since not all kinds of emotion are appropriate for expression to God, not all kinds of music are appropriate either.

Finally, all of our musical choices matter, because all music shapes our affections. We've focused in this chapter on sacred music, but even music with non-sacred texts shapes our spirits and either prevents us from being able to rightly appreciate good music or helps us develop the right kinds of affections.

If you have always viewed sacred music as merely an enjoyable way to affirm biblical truth, perhaps you need to adjust your thinking to recognize the great power and importance of music in worship.

chapter four

How Should We Evaluate Musical Communication?

"THERE IS NOTHING UN-CHRISTIAN or anti-Christian about any kind of music."[14]

So says Harold Best, Dean Emeritus of Music at Wheaton College. He later re-emphasized that, "The Christian is free of the moral nothingness of music."[15]

This is not an uncommon sentiment among Christians today. In fact, it is probably the most common belief of modern Christians. But does this view that music is completely neutral stand against the teachings of Scripture and an understanding of the science of music?

Musical Communication in the Bible

Many proponents of the neutrality of music argue that since the Bible does not explicitly say that music communicates, then it does not. Not only is this a faulty view of biblical interpretation and application, but also the Bible does imply musical communication in several instances.

Worship that Sounds Like War

One of the first examples in Scripture of music communicating a recognizable message is in Exodus 32. Moses is on Mt. Sinai receiving the Ten Commandments from the Lord with Joshua waiting just down the way. After receiving the tables of the Law, Moses and Joshua begin to make their way back down the mountain to the camp of the Israelites. As they near the camp, Joshua hears a noise. "There is a noise of war in the camp," he tells Moses as he likely reaches for his sword (v. 17).

But Moses knows better. You see, before returning down the mountain, the Lord himself had told Moses that his people had turned from him and begun worshiping an idol. Moses knows that what Joshua heard with his younger ears was not the sound of war, but the sound of worship — worship of Yahweh using pagan methods. This is not the sound of victory or defeat in war; this is music. But what is important for our purposes is that the music that the Israelites were using in their worship communicated a very clear message to Joshua, a message of chaos and turmoil — a message Joshua associated with war.

This account does not explicitly teach anything about music *per se*, but it does imply that music can communicate messages and therefore very strongly suggest certain associations to our minds.

Refreshing the Spirit

Perhaps the most well-known passage about the effects of music is 1 Samuel 16:1—23. King Saul has disobeyed God and forfeited the throne and David has been anointed King of Israel. In verse 14 we read, "Now the Spirit of the LORD departed from Saul, and a harmful spirit from the LORD tormented him."

Notice the contrast between two kinds of "spirits" — the "Spirit of the Lord" and a "harmful spirit from the Lord." The "Spirit of the Lord" is definitely the Holy Spirit and most likely refers to the special anointing that God's earthly representatives enjoyed in the Old Testament economy. Once Saul lost his right to be King, that special anointing of the Holy Spirit left him.

In the place of the Holy Spirit, Saul is now overcome with "a harmful spirit from the Lord." There is some disagreement over exactly what this "spirit" was. Some take the position that this was a demonic spirit that tormented Saul, and that is a possibility.

But since this spirit is "from the Lord," it is more likely that this term refers to a mental or emotional condition. In other words, "spirit" refers to Saul's own spirit. The phrase could correctly be translated, "Saul was overcome by a troubled spirit from the Lord." In other words, in place of his special anointing upon Saul, God caused Saul to be overcome with a disturbed emotional condition.

So Saul is experiencing some kind of troubled emotional state that worries his servants and motivates them to look for a solution. His servants know that troubled emotions can often be soothed through calming, beautiful music, and so Saul sends for David to play upon his harp. And as David played, "Saul's spirit was refreshed" (v. 23).

What this passage implies is that music can communicate messages to our spirits — to our emotions — in such a way that it actually changes our emotions. When we are experiencing a depressed or troubled emotional condition, music that communicates peace and serenity can soothe us and change our emotions.

Instrumental Emotion

The Bible contains several other passages that imply musical communication:

> Therefore my harp is tuned to mourning, and my flute to the sound of those who weep (Job 30:31).

> Therefore my heart intones like a harp for Moab and my inward feelings for Kir-hareseth (Isaiah 16:11).

Therefore my heart wails for Moab like flutes; my heart also wails like flutes for the men of Kir-heres (Jeremiah 48:36).

In other words, the Bible uses the sounds of musical instruments as metaphors to describe certain emotional states. A harp can be played to sound like human mourning or weeping, or a flute can be played to communicate wailing and other troubling emotions. These are emotions that all people in all times and places share.

Emotional Metaphor

So the Bible in several places implies that instrumental music, without any words, can communicate emotional messages, but it does not tell us what kinds of music communicate certain messages or even how it works. To discover how and what music communicates, we must look to the science of music itself.

Music is a medium of communication. In particular, music communicates by means of emotional metaphor. In other words, by using symbols, music can communicate various moods and emotions. Symbols are essentially associations. X is *like* Y, so X can *represent* Y. My love is like a red, red rose because my love reminds me of the beauty and delicacy of a rose, and therefore, I associate my beautiful, delicate love with a rose. In this sense, all musical communication is based on association. The music is not emotion; it is merely symbols of emotion. It does not create emotion; it expresses ideas of emotion. Music communicates certain moods and emotions to us because we associate its symbols with various emotional states.

Conventional Association

Some symbolism is purely association with man-made conventions. The colors red, white, and blue possess no inherent association with American patriotism, but since they are the colors of our flag, such colors possess symbolic representation of pride in our nation. Raising your arm at a straight, 45° angle in front of your body does not possess inherent association with fascism and tyranny, but because such a bodily gesture was the Nazi salute to Hitler, it carries with it symbolic representation of terrible times.

Some musical communication occurs because of these kinds of conventional associations. Sometimes these associations are true for particular individuals or small groups; other times these associations exist for entire cultures or time periods. Sometimes such associations eventually fade away, while in some few cases they last for a long period of time. This is the "Honey, they're playing our song" phenomenon.

For instance, the final section of Rossini's overture to the opera *William Tell* is often associated with a masked "Lone Ranger" riding his horse Silver. There is nothing, of course, inherent in this music without lyrics to automatically suggest such a picture, but because those musical phrases were used as the theme for the Lone Ranger show, we associate those musical symbols with such images.

I once heard of an American missionary in Great Britain who used "Glorious Things of Thee Are Spoken" one Sunday in a service. As soon as the hymn began, an older British gentlemen stood up in a huff and stormed out of the room. Later, the missionary discovered that the man was a World War II veteran who associated the tune of that song, which was the tune of the German national anthem, with the Nazis who had ruthlessly bombed his country. There was nothing inherent in the tune to offend the gentleman; he simply associated it with terrible times from his past.

Natural Association

On the other hand, some symbolism is natural association. Dark clouds naturally signify a storm because they

63

naturally accompany a storm. A symbol of a lightning bolt naturally signifies electricity because it is the shape naturally associated with electricity. A frown naturally signifies sadness because it naturally accompanies the feeling of sadness. In order for symbolic meaning to be natural, the association between the symbol and the object must occur naturally in human experience.

Some musical communication occurs because of these kinds of natural associations. Combinations of dynamics, tone colors, rhythms, and tempos can combine to mimic the natural way we feel inwardly or physically respond outwardly when we experience certain emotional states.

For instance, there is a reason Pachelbel's *Canon in D Major* is played on peaceful, serene occasions like the prelude to a wedding and not before a football game; the musical symbols naturally communicate peace and serenity — not pep and excitement — because they mimic how we feel when we are peaceful. There is a reason Sousa marches are played at football games and not at weddings; the musical symbols naturally communicate rousing enthusiasm appropriate for a sporting event and not a marriage ceremony. There is a reason a Pink Floyd song is going to be played at a strip club and not Pachelbel's *Canon* or a Sousa march; the musical symbols naturally communicate the kinds of feelings occurring there.

Perhaps the best illustration of this kind of natural symbolic communication in music is with film scores. Certain musical scores are composed for movie scenes based on the kinds of moods and emotions the producers want to enhance with the given scene, and they know that such communication will occur with any audience regardless of age, demographic, nationality, gender or culture because all humans share basic emotional and physical makeup. When movies are shown in different countries, the spoken language changes, but the music doesn't.

Music is often referred to as "heightened speech." Musical forms evolved over time as more complex forms of natural emotional intonation. In other words, there is a natural connection between musical communication and what naturally occurs with our voices as we experience certain emotional states. In this way natural symbols are transcultural, because every man shares a culture of humanity.

So how does this help us with our musical choices? Specific musical styles or individual songs always possess some natural meanings and often possess various conventional meanings, both by way of symbolic association. At the very heart of all musical meaning is the natural meaning it communicates by way of its association with universal, common human experience. But built upon that natural meaning are various conventional associations. Often such conventional associations will correspond to the natural meaning, as with the natural expressions of peacefulness communicated by Pachelbel's Canon that give rise to the conventional association of that particular piece with weddings, or such as the natural expressions of sexuality communicated by Pink Floyd that give rise to the conventional associations of that music to immoral living.

Sometimes, however, conventional associations can contradict and override natural associations. For instance, although the tune of "Glorious Things of Thee Are Spoken" naturally communicates noble moods because of its natural association with how we feel when we are proud or stately, its conventional association with Nazi Germany created new meaning during WWII that overpowered the positive meaning with that was quite negative.

In summary, music communicates through symbolic associations, and such associations can be either conventional or natural depending upon whether or not they correspond to something that occurs naturally in all human experience.

Add a lyric to a musical selection, and we now have two additional layers of meaning: the obvious content of the text and the poetic "mood." What must be remembered here is that symbolic meaning (in this case, music), if it is natural, always trumps the text. For instance, if I were to approach my wife with a frown, furrowed brow, and loud tone of voice (natural symbols of anger) and say to her, "I love you," my negative body language and tone of voice would surely overpower the potential positive meaning of the statement. At very least she would think I was making some kind of joke.

For very practical purposes of making musical choices in our lives, it really doesn't matter whether musical communication is conventional or natural. The important question to ask as you make musical choices is, "What does that music communicate on an emotional level? Does it sound sad? Does it sound happy? Does it sound chaotic? Does it sound sexual?"

But even in asking questions like these, we need to be careful not to limit emotional meaning to only the broad categories signified by words like joy, love, or aggression. Remember, mere words are inadequate to perfectly express the nuances of emotions since even within a category like "joy," there are lots of different kinds of joy. We must not only ask, "What does that music communicate?" We must also ask, "What *kind* of joy or love or aggression does it communicate?"

Evaluating Musical Communication

From both Scriptural implication and an understanding of the science of music, it is clear that music does communicate. Therefore, in making musical choices, we must be willing to apply all of the Bible's instruction about communication to those choices.

Perhaps one of the most concise passages about communication in Scripture is Ephesians 4:29:

> Let no corrupting talk come out of your mouths, but only such as is good for building up, as fits the occasion, that it may give grace to those who hear.

This passage most directly addresses our verbal speech, but it certainly applies to other forms of communication including writing, body language, gestures, facial expressions, and art forms like music. Each of these are means of human communication, and so each of these fall under the authority of passages like Ephesians 4:29.

Corrupt Communication

Paul exhorts that we are not to let any corrupt communication come from us. The term translated "corrupting" has the idea of something that is rotten, foul, or putrid. It was often used to describe rotting plants or fruits. It clearly refers to any kind of communication that is sinful or spiritually harmful. For a Christian, these kinds of messages shouldn't "even be named among [us]" (Ephesians 5:3).

The most obvious part of our musical choices where this applies is the lyrics of songs we listen to or sing, but I'm amazed at how many Christians tolerate (or enjoy!) songs with lyrics that not only hint at sin but outright approve of sin! As Christians, we must reject songs that talk about or imply sinful deeds even through innuendo. We must avoid songs that talk about "sexual immorality, impurity, sensuality, idolatry, sorcery, enmity, strife, jealousy, fits of anger, rivalries, dissensions, divisions, envy, drunkenness, orgies, *and things like these*" (Galatians 5:19—21). Even things like "foolish talk" or "crude joking" are "out of place" for the Christian (Ephesians 5:4).

But our evaluation of music does not end with the lyrics of songs. Since music is a medium of communication through the use of emotional metaphors, music can communicate the kinds of emotions that naturally represent sinful deeds. There are certain kinds of emotions that naturally accompany sexual immorality, impurity, strife, fits of anger, drunkenness, orgies, *and things like these*. And just as we must avoid those sinful acts, we must avoid the emotions and moods that accompany those acts.

Someone might argue that there is no such thing as sinful emotion — emotion only becomes sinful when it is accompanied by sin. They might use the emotion of anger, for example, and argue that anger is sometimes good and sometimes bad; it just depends upon the context.

However, remember again that words are merely feeble attempts to identify spiritual realities. The term "anger" is a very broad category that does not adequately specify particular *kinds* of anger in that broader category. So the anger that accompanies a noble cause is *a different kind of anger* than that which accompanies vengeance. In order to more exactly specify the difference, we might call the first kind "righteous indignation" and the latter kind "unbridled rage." We're not just using different words to signify when "neutral" anger accompanies good or evil acts. We are actually describing two *different kinds* of anger, one that is always good and one that is always evil. And music can actually communicate the difference between these kinds of anger in ways that mere words may not be able.

Why must we avoid expressions of emotion that naturally accompany sinful acts? First, by exposing ourselves to music that communicates the kinds of emotions that naturally fit with sin, we are tacitly approving those sins. We may not actually be committing those sins, but we are at the very least letting those sins "be named among [us]" (Ephesians 5:3) as we participate in the music.

But even more importantly, by exposing ourselves to musical communication that accompanies sinful works, we are corrupting our own morals. 1 Corinthians 15:33 gives us the principle: "Do not be deceived: 'Bad company ruins good morals.'"

Any parent knows that if he allows his child to hang around with other children who are involved in overt sinful behavior, eventually the morals of his own child will be ruined. And so parents protect their children by guarding what influences their children's lives.

Listening to music is like hanging around with people. Just like people's moods and morals "rub off" on those who keep company with them, so the emotions and moods communicated by music "rub off" on people who listen to it. Therefore, bad music ruins good morals.

As Christians, we must avoid all kinds of communication that are corrupt. This includes sinful words of lyrics and sinful emotions of music.

Edifying Communication

Rather, a Christian's communication must be edifying — it must "build up" others and even ourselves (Ephesians 4:29). Again, this command applies equally to the words of lyrics and the emotional messages of music. Listening to music that expresses noble affections is a way of approving what is good, and "good music promotes good morals."

As Christians, we must not fill our lives with sinful actions or attitudes, but neither should we fill our lives with things we might simply consider "neutral." Rather, as Paul argues in 1 Corinthians 10:23, "'All things are lawful,' but not all things are helpful. 'All things are lawful,'" but not all things build up.'"

In other words, Paul is saying that we shouldn't be content even with things that are simply "lawful" or "acceptable." As Christians, we should look for things that are helpful, beneficial, profitable, and edifying. We should not be asking, "What's wrong with it?" We should be asking, "What is *right* with it?"

This includes our musical choices. We should chose songs with lyrics and music that communicate noble messages. This doesn't necessarily mean that it has to be "sacred." Music that talks about general things of life or even music with no lyrics at all can express noble, beneficial, edifying messages. Again, we must ask, "What does this music communicate?"

Evaluating whether a song expresses corrupt communication or edifying communication should create two clear categories for a Christian — one category from which he may choose and one he should avoid. This assertion does not imply that musical evaluation is easy or that the issue is as "black and white" as some wish it were. But if a Christian is willing to make the effort to evaluate his musical choices based upon the guidelines about communication in God's Word, he should be able to group songs and styles into one of those two categories. Then, within the category of music that expresses edifying messages, a Christian has great liberty for preference.

Musical Communication Choices

Corrupt	Edifying
Avoid At All Times	Room for Preferences

Fitting Communication

Yet this is not where a Christian's musical evaluation may stop. Even having created these two categories in his mind, he must then consider the appropriateness of a song or style for a given situation. He must ask, "Is this song or style fitting for this circumstance?"

Even good songs or styles may be inappropriate for certain circumstances. Brahm's "Lullaby" is an edifying piece of music, but it certainly would not be fitting to play at a pep rally before a sporting event. A John Philip Sousa march is an edifying piece of music, but I wouldn't play it to put my infant daughter to sleep!

Likewise, when we consider the kind of music we will use for sacred purposes, we must consider whether even something that is inherently good is also *fitting*. Here is where we must carefully consider nuanced differences between *kinds* of emotions. We are to rejoice in the Lord, certainly, but there is a kind of "joy" that is not what Paul was talking about in Philippians 4:4. Paul did not have in mind a kind of flippant, care-free frivolity. Other qualities expressed throughout Scripture must characterize spiritual joy, things like reverence, sobriety, and gravity. We are to love the Lord our God with our entire being, but there is a kind of "love" that is not worthy of the Lord. Since music can express these different nuanced emotions, we must evaluate whether what a certain song or style is communicating is appropriate for expressing God's truth.

Musical Communication Choices

Corrupt	Edifying	
	Fitting	Unfitting
Avoid At All Times	Room for Preferences	Avoid For This Occasion

Why must we consider the fittingness of musical style for sacred purposes? Why is musical style important at all? Biblical truth is important, the gospel is important, but musical style?

It is certainly true that the most important things to a Christian are the gospel and biblical truth. These are the center of our attention and devotion.

But evaluating a musical style that carries biblical truth is just as important as being concerned about what kind of dish we use to serve a gourmet meal to an honored guest. Really, the dishes aren't the most important thing — the food is! We want to make certain that we serve the best food possible to our guest. Yet the dish is important because if we were to serve prime rib on a dirty paper plate, the food itself would be ruined. We concern ourselves with the dish because we love the food. Actually, even the food is important only as it relates to our guest.

The same is true as we consider the musical dishes upon which we serve the sacred food of God's truth. The truth is what is most important, but the dish can either enhance or harm the food.

Our criteria become even more narrowed as we consider what kind of music we will use in corporate worship. Here is a time of focused, congregational adoration of God through presentations of truth and spiritual response, and we must be certain that the musical styles we are choosing are fitting for this sacred time.

Conventional Associations

Finally, we must also consider the conventional associations a song or style have even after we have judged it to be edifying in and of itself. Paul discusses this issue in 1 Corinthians with relation to meat that had been offered to idols.

Controversy had arisen in the church in Corinth over whether or not it was appropriate for Christians to eat meat that had been previously offered in pagan worship ceremonies. Paul's judgment of the controversy is that the meat in and of itself is good; it is beneficial. There is nothing inherently evil about meat that has been sacrificed to a false god since the god doesn't really exist (1 Corinthians 8:4ff).

However, at the end of the chapter, Paul declares that he will not eat the meat. Why would he refuse to eat something that he has judged to be good? He gives two primary reasons.

First, Paul knows that some weaker Christians may be led to stumble into sin if they see someone stronger than they indulging in such meat. The meat carries a conventional association with pagan worship and the immoral activities that occur there, and someone without adequate understanding may interpret indulgence of the meat by stronger Christians as an endorsement of the practices of pagan worship. The problem is not with the meat; the problem is that uninformed Christians are strongly impacted by conventional associations. Paul's decision is that if indulging in something may cause someone weaker to stumble into sin, he is willing to give it up:

> But take care that this right of yours does not somehow become a stumbling block to the weak. [10]For if anyone sees you who have knowledge eating in an idol's temple, will he not be encouraged, if his conscience is weak, to eat food offered to idols? [11]And so by your knowledge this weak person is destroyed, the brother for whom Christ died. [12]Thus, sinning against your brothers and wounding their conscience when it is weak, you sin against Christ. [13]Therefore, if food makes my brother stumble, I will never eat meat, lest I make my brother stumble (1 Corinthians 8:9—13).

This applies to musical choices when a certain song or style is so strongly associated with a particular sinful lifestyle that someone less spiritually mature than you might stumble into sin because of your indulgence. And remember, the "weaker brothers" over which many of us have continual influence are our children.

The second reason Paul is willing to give up a legitimate right is for the sake of the gospel. For this point Paul uses the issues of freedom to marry and to be paid for one's ministry as examples. Paul argues in 1 Corinthians 9 that he has every right to financial support by the churches (v. 4), the right to marriage (v. 5), and the right to exemption from manual labor (v. 6). However, Paul insists that he will make "no use of any of these rights" (v. 15). Why? He was removing anything that could possibly hinder the progress of the gospel. It is in this sense that he becomes "all things to all people, that by all means [he] might save some" (v. 22). It is not that he compromised or was willing to indulge in otherwise questionable activities in order to appeal to certain people.

Paul was willing to remove any possible stumbling block lest it hinder the gospel. He says, "I do it all for the sake of the gospel, that I may share with them in its blessings" (v. 23).

Evidently receiving money from churches, taking a wife, and refraining from manual labor each carried certain conventional associations in that day that would have presented difficulties for evangelism. Paul says that if that's a possibility, he is willing to refrain.

This principle would apply to musical choices when an otherwise good song or musical style would hinder evangelistic endeavors because of some kind of conventional association. A mark of spiritual maturity is a freedom to give up a legitimate right for the sake of others.

Musical Communication Choices

Corrupt	Edifying		
	Fitting		Unfitting
Avoid At All Times	Negative Association	Positive Association	Avoid For This Occasion
	Avoid For This Occasion	Room for Preferences	

Conclusion

Evaluating musical meaning is important because all meaning is important. How and what we communicate matters, and therefore, means of communication like music matter.

The Bible implies musical communication, the science of music explains musical communication, and it is up to us to discern the meaning, appropriateness, and associations of songs and styles and make informed decisions about whether we should choose to use them.

chapter five

Is Beauty in the Eye of the Beholder?

IMAGINE I TELL MY WIFE that I want to take her to a special place for our anniversary. We arrange for a babysitter for our children, we dress in our finest clothes, and we hop into our car to set off for our romantic "mystery" destination.

Becky's excitement soon turns to bewilderment as I pull into the local junk yard. I park the car, open the trunk, and pull out a small table and chairs. I proceed to set up the table, putting a candle in the middle, place settings on each side, and a picnic basket next to the table.

"Here we are, dear," I exclaim, "all set for our romantic dinner."

"A romantic dinner in a *junk yard*?" Becky questions.

"Sure," I answer. "I thought this place would set the mood nicely. Don't you just love how the rust on the scrap metal glimmers in the lowering sunlight and how the smell of garbage adds that extra touch to our evening?"

"No, I don't," she replies with a frown. "I don't find this setting pleasing at all."

"Oh, come on, " I object. "Beauty is in the eye of the

beholder, isn't it? You just need to re-adjust your perceptions."

The situation is silly, of course. No one in their right mind would consider a junk yard beautiful or romantic. There are certain smells and sights that are objectively *ugly*!

Yet in a culture of relativism, the scenario above sounds strangely plausible. If people do not believe in absolute standards by which to determine beauty, who is to say that a junk yard is not beautiful?

A Christian believes in absolute standards of truth and righteousness. Such standards may be discerned from the Word of God and the nature and character of God.

But what about absolute standards of beauty? Do they exist?

The idea of "beauty" traditionally describes an object or idea in which we take pleasure simply for what it is. In other words, if we delight in something for what it can *do* for us, we don't necessarily call that thing "beautiful." We call something like that "good." We call something beautiful when we take pleasure in it apart from any practical benefit we may receive from it. A beautiful object has intrinsic qualities in it that cause delight.

For example, I take pleasure in my computer because

it allows me to accomplish a lot of things, but I wouldn't call my computer "beautiful." On the other hand, I take pleasure in watching a sunset even though it does absolutely nothing for me. It is this kind of delightful thing that I would call "beautiful."

Is this notion of "beauty" found in Scripture?

In order to answer this question, we must first recognize that although we commonly use the term "beauty" today in signifying this concept, biblical authors use many different terms to describe this same idea. In your English translation you might find the idea of beauty encapsulated in words like *sweetness*, *splendor*, *majesty*, *pride*, *excellence*, *loveliness*, *purity*, *admirability*, *glory*, or even *goodness*. Words like these are often translations of Hebrew or Greek terms that resemble our idea of "beauty."

The Source of Beauty

Essential to a definition of beauty is pleasure. People call something beautiful because of the pleasure they find in it apart from what it can do for them.

The Beauty of God

God himself is the one in Scripture most commonly associated with delight and pleasure. For example, notice the joy and delight God's people find in God in the following passages:

> You make known to me the path of life; in your presence there is **fullness of joy**; at your right hand are **pleasures** forevermore (Psalm 16:11).

> Then I will go to the altar of God, to God my **exceeding joy**, and I will praise you with the lyre, O God, my God (Psalm 43:4).

> You **satisfy the desire** of every living thing (Psalm 145:16).

In each of these cases, God's people do not find joy in him because of what he can *do* for them, although his works are certainly great and worthy of delight. Rather, God's people delight in him simply because of who he is, because of qualities intrinsic to his nature.

What are these intrinsic qualities? Notice the words used to describe God in the following passages:

> And when he had consulted with the people, he appointed those who should sing to the LORD, and who should praise the **beauty** of holiness (2 Chronicles 20:21).

> Have you an arm like God? Or can you thunder with a voice like his? [10]Then adorn yourself with **majesty** and **splendor**, and array yourself with **glory** and

beauty (Job 40:9—10).

O LORD, our Lord, how **excellent** is your name in all the earth, who have set your **glory** above the heavens (Psalm 8:1)!

One thing I have desired of the LORD, that will I seek: That I may dwell in the house of the LORD all the days of my life, to behold the **beauty** of the LORD, and to inquire in his temple (Psalm 27:4).

I will meditate on the **glorious splendor** of your **majesty**, and on Your wondrous works (Psalm 145:5).

They shall see the **glory** of the LORD, the **excellency** of our God (Isaiah 35:2).

For how great is his goodness and how great his **beauty** (Zechariah 9:17)!

God is called "beautiful," "glorious," "majestic," and "full of splendor." These are qualities inherent to the nature of God and qualities in which his people delight.

So here we find the essential concept of "beauty" used to characterize God himself. God has unique qualities that bring pleasure to people separate from what he does for them. God is Beauty.

But I want you to notice something further in Scripture about this pleasure in God who is beautiful. Finding pleasure in God is not optional. God's people are commanded to find joy in him:

> **Delight** yourself in the LORD, and he will give you the desires of your heart (Psalm 37:4).

> **Rejoice** in the Lord always; again I will say, **Rejoice** (Philippians 4:4).

What this means is that these qualities of beauty inherent in God's nature and character are *worthy* of pleasure; they must be delighted in. Failure to delight in God for his inherent excellence is tantamount to sin. Another way of saying it is this: it is not pleasure in God that *makes* him beautiful. It is objective qualities of beauty that *require* pleasure. These qualities in God are absolute standards of beauty.

In Scripture, this necessity to delight in God because of his intrinsic worth is called *glorifying God* or *praising God*. To glorify or praise God is to find joy in him because of qualities in his nature that are worthy of such delight.

The Beauty of Creation

The beauty of God then extends to his creation. In Genesis 1 God calls his creation "good" (Genesis 1:4, 10, 12, 18, 21, and 25), a word that has implications of beauty. Creation puts on display of the beauty of God:

> The heavens declare the **glory** of God, and the sky above proclaims his handiwork (Psalm 19:1).

What God created may be considered beautiful because it reflects and displays his beauty. In other words, the same qualities that make God beautiful are those standards by which his creation may be considered beautiful.

Further, God calls certain man-made creations "beautiful," as well. For example, God commands Israel to build his Tabernacle (and later, the Temple) to display beauty. In prescribing how he wants the priestly garments made, God says,

> For Aaron's sons you shall make coats and sashes and caps. You shall make them for **glory and beauty** (Exodus 28:40).

So even men can create things that are beautiful. Again, these human creations may be considered beautiful inasmuch as they possess qualities that reflect the beautiful qualities of God.

This is all important as we seek to discover whether absolute standards of beauty exist. The notion that "beauty is in the eye of the beholder" flows from a kind of thinking that says, "Whatever I find pleasurable is beautiful to me."

Yet as we have seen from the beauty of God, something does not *become* beautiful simply because someone delights in it. Something *is* beautiful because of its qualities whether or not people find it pleasurable. A sunset *is* beautiful whether or not someone acknowledges the fact. And it is therefore possible to delight in something and think it is beautiful when it is in fact not beautiful.

Absolute standards of beauty exist, and they are found in the very nature of God.

Qualities of Beauty

What, then, are these qualities intrinsic to the nature of God that serve as the absolute standards of beauty? We can find such qualities from three sources.

First, we can discern qualities of God's beauty from descriptions of his nature. Divine attributes such as holiness, purity, reason, harmony, order, balance, goodness, majesty, splendor, righteousness, and loveliness provide the qualities that we should delight in and emulate. Second, since God's own handiwork displays his beauty, we may look to qualities within creation to determine standards of beauty. Romans 1:20 tells us that God's invisible attributes, such as his attribute of beauty, may be perceived in creation. Third, since God calls certain man-made creations beautiful in Scripture, we may use them as models for what is beautiful.

When considering both God's beautiful creative works and the works of man to which God ascribes beauty, theologians have long categorized absolute standards of beauty into three groupings: (1) order, (2) proportion, and (3) radiance.

The Marring of Beauty

If not for the presence of sin, all creation would still be beautiful, and by extension all creations of man would also be beautiful. Yet sin subjected creation to futility (Romans 8:20), and thus sin brought ugliness into the world. Because of sin we now have *dis*-order, *dis*-proportion, and dullness. Just as something is beautiful when it rightly reflects the qualities of God that make him beautiful, so something is ugly when it possesses qualities contrary to the nature of God. The presence of sin in our own hearts (Jeremiah 17:9) is the reason we cannot simply trust ourselves to determine what is beautiful. We must look to absolute standards outside ourselves. Sin is also the reason we must carefully judge all man-made creations, including music.

Remembering that the idea of beauty is encapsulated in the biblical concept of "glory," we can see the relationship between sin and ugliness in passages like Romans 3:23: "For all have sinned and fall short of the glory of God." To fall short of God's glory is to fail in delighting in God as we should.

There are two primary ways that we can fail to bring God glory in this area. First, when we delight in something to a more fundamental degree than we delight in God, we fall short of his glory. Glorifying God is delighting in his unique excellencies. To take delight in something else to the same or greater degree is sin. Likewise, when we fail to take delight in God at all for his unique qualities, we fall short of his glory. God described this kind of sin when he said through Jeremiah,

> For my people have committed two evils: they have forsaken me, the fountain of living waters, and hewed out cisterns for themselves, broken cisterns that can hold no water (Jeremiah 2:13).

Second, when we delight in something that possesses qualities contrary to the nature of God, we also fail to bring God glory. To call something beautiful that is not is

92

to contradict the beauty of God himself.

This is why distinguishing between the beautiful and the ugly is so important. To call something ugly that is beautiful when compared to God is to call God ugly. To call something beautiful that is ugly when compared to God is also calling God ugly.

Let me illustrate it this way. My wife has beautifully decorated our home. If I were to proclaim, "These decorations are ugly," what would I be saying about my opinion of my wife's decorations? Likewise, if I were to say, "I think it's much more beautiful to decorate with graffiti on the walls and bouquets of dirty socks," would I not also be saying something significant about my opinion of my wife's decorating?

Glorifying God is taking delight in him because of qualities in his nature. Therefore in order to glorify him, we must also delight in other things that resemble him and despise things that do not resemble him.

The Redemption of Beauty

Since sin marred beauty in creation, the atoning work of Christ on the cross and subsequent regeneration of individuals by the Holy Spirit is the way in which man's capacity to correctly take pleasure in God and other things worthy of such delight is redeemed. Because of sin, every man is born without the capacity to delight in God (Romans 3:10—12), yet because men are God's creation, they are born with an innate need to delight in something. This causes them to spend their lives finding ultimate satisfaction in things that are not God and things that are inherently ugly.

The gospel of Jesus Christ provides the supernatural means by which people are enabled to see the beauty of God in the person of Christ. We find this explained in 2 Corinthians 4:3—6:

> And even if our gospel is veiled, it is veiled only to those who are perishing. [4]In their case the god of this world has blinded the minds of the unbelievers, to keep them from seeing the light of the gospel of the glory of Christ, who is the image of God. [5]For what we proclaim is not ourselves, but Jesus Christ as Lord, with ourselves as your servants for Jesus' sake. [6]For God, who said, "Let light shine out of darkness," has shone in our hearts to give the light of the knowledge of the glory of God in the face of Jesus Christ.

Veiled Beauty

Unbelievers cannot apprehend the beauty of the gospel and of Christ. This is what the text means in verse 4 when it says that they do not see "the light of the gospel of the glory of Christ." They do not perceive its wonders and its value and its beauty, and therefore they do not submit to the gospel since they do not recognize its value.

We submit to things only when we appreciate their value, not when we simply know about them or believe in them with our minds. We follow after what we delight in, not just what we know.

Here's an example. My wife once spent a considerable amount of time searching for a rug for our living room. She enjoyed doing it. She knew in her mind that our living room needed a rug, but that was not what compelled her to search intently to find just the right rug. *I* knew in *my* mind that our living room needed a rug, but that knowledge certainly did not compel *me* to spend hours looking for one. In essence, Becky finds pleasure in the beauty of rugs; I see only their practical worth. Since Becky recognized the beauty and value of a rug, she was willing to spend time committed to finding one.

Someone may understand the facts of the gospel, but unless he recognizes the beauty and value of the gospel, he will not submit to it.

Revealed Beauty

Yet there is hope. Just like God created beauty at the

beginning, so he has the power to illumine hearts so that they apprehend the beauty of the gospel. And when he does this, when God illuminates the heart, then the beauty of the gospel of the glory of Christ is revealed!

It's as if men are groping around in a pitch black cave desperately searching for the treasure that they know to be there but cannot find. And then suddenly a spotlight is shown directly in front of them to reveal a magnificent diamond that was there the whole time.

All men are born in blackness. They are blinded as to the beauty of the gospel of Christ. They are empty, they are searching. In their heart of hearts they know that there must be something that will satisfy their longings, something that will fill the void in their souls. But they are unwilling and unable to accept that it is God himself who will satisfy that longing, God himself who will fill that void. All they must do is submit to God as King and they will find that treasure. But they hate God, and they reject their knowledge of him. They are unwilling to submit to the gospel because they do not recognize the beauty of the glory of Jesus Christ.

But then, just as God created light at the beginning of time, with just his voice he says, "Let there be light," and light shines on a dark heart. And when that happens, that perishing person looks up and sees the truths of the gospel literally in a new light. No more does he see mere facts about a man who once lived and died. No longer does he see God as ugly. No longer does he see the demands of the gospel as unreasonable. That light that has been shined upon his heart reveals the magnificent beauty of the gospel of the glory of Jesus Christ.

Jesus Christ is the ultimate expression of the beauty of God because he is the very image of God. John 1:14 says, "And the Word became flesh and dwelt among us, and we have seen his glory [or beauty], glory as of the only Son from the Father, full of grace and truth." Hebrews 1:3 tells us that Christ is "the radiance of the glory [or beauty] of God and the exact imprint of his nature."

Regeneration restores in an individual the ability to recognize what is truly beautiful, first in the person of Jesus Christ, and then in other things. This does not mean that unbelievers cannot recognize beauty or even create beauty. God's common grace enables even the unregenerate to do so.

But what this means is that a believer has no excuse when it comes to making value judgments about beauty.

The Judgment of Beauty

Once a person becomes a Christian — once his capacity to recognize beauty has been restored — that person has an obligation to correctly judge things beautiful or ugly. God commands believers to "test everything" and "hold fast to that which is good" (1 Thessalonians 5:21). The word translated "good" here signifies the intrinsic excellencies of something, and its first definition in Greek dictionaries is "beautiful." It is contrasted with "good" from verse 15 of the same passage, a word that identifies something that is beneficial. In other words, here Christians are specifically commanded to evaluate everything in order to determine whether something has intrinsic worth.

The Good, the Bad, and the Ugly

Perhaps the passage that most clearly articulates such a command is Philippians 4:8:

> Finally, brothers, whatever is true, whatever is honorable, whatever is just, whatever is pure, whatever is lovely, whatever is commendable, if there is any excellence, if there is anything worthy of praise, think about these things.

Here we find a list of absolute standards by which we

must judge all things. The phrase rendered "think about" literally means, "take into account." Everything we encounter must be judged by the qualities in this list. Each of these terms is worth considering:

- "true" — truthful, honest, real, genuine
- "honorable" — noble, of good character, worthy
- "just" — conforming to the standard, righteous
- "pure" — holy, chaste, innocent
- "lovely" — literally "towards affection," pleasing
- "commendable" — worthy of praise, admirable
- "excellence" — moral excellence
- "worthy of praise" — commendation, approval

These qualities could be grouped into the three categories of truth, goodness, and beauty. Something is true when it agrees with reality; something is good when it meets real needs; and something is beautiful when it is worthy of pleasure.

In all three of these categories, there is a subjective realm (what we think) and an objective realm (what really is). With truth, we may subjectively think something is true that is objectively not true. For example, I may truly believe that grass is red, but that doesn't make it true. So in the case of truth, we must always change what we think is true to match what God says is true in his Word. John 17:17 says, "Sanctify them in the truth; your word is truth." With my belief about the color of grass, I have to readjust my beliefs to match reality.

With goodness, we may subjectively think that something is good for us when it is objectively not good. For example, I may think that drinking cyanide daily is good for me, but that doesn't make it so. Here, too, we must always change what we think is good to match what God says is good. With my views of cyanide, either I would need to adjust my thinking or reality would eventually sink in!

The same is true with beauty. We may subjectively think something is beautiful — we may take pleasure in something — but what we think may not match with what is objectively beautiful. For example, I may take pleasure in a particular work of art or song or style of music and think that it is beautiful, but that does not make it beautiful. According to this passage, we are to take into account things that are worthy of praise, things that are *admirable*. This implies absolute standards. Here again we must change our tastes to match what God says is beautiful. Our responsibility as Christians is to change what we take pleasure in to those things that are actually *worthy* of our pleasure — those thing that are actually beautiful.

Change Your Taste

During the years I was in college and the one year before I was married, I ate a lot of junk food. I grew to love junk food. So when I eventually married, and my wife began to prepare healthy, well-balanced meals for me, I'll admit that I really didn't have a taste for it at first!

But over time, after abstaining from junk and dieting on healthy cuisine, I soon developed a taste for that which was actually good.

Similarly, Christians can change their tastes to match what is actually worthy of their delight. There are three truths about the Christian life that if you come to understand will really help you in this realm of beauty:

1. We like what we know. Some people think, "Well, I happen to like that, and there's nothing I can do about it." That is simply not true. We develop a taste for things we regularly feed ourselves. We like what we're accustomed to.

2. We can change what we like by changing what we know. Unbelievers are constrained to do what they like, but not believers. Christians have freedom in Christ to give things up even if they really like them. And Christians have freedom to bring things into their lives that they might not really like at first.

3. *As Christians, we have an obligation to like what is worthy of liking.* We have the responsibility to judge all things and evaluate whether something is worthy of our delight based upon absolute standards about the nature and character of God. If we determine something to be unworthy, we have an obligation to call it what it is and rid ourselves of it. And if we determine something to be truly worthy, then our delight in that thing magnifies our delight in him who is ultimately beautiful.

chapter six

How Should We Think About Sunday Morning?

THE SCENE IS ALL TOO FAMILIAR. The alarm goes off on Sunday morning. After hitting the snooze button one or two times, you finally crawl out of bed to begin a hectic morning of getting yourself and the rest of your family ready for the morning service with your church.

You scramble around to get clean, decide what you're going to wear, scarf down a piece of toast, and find that missing shoe. After a hurried trip down the road, you race into the church building and plop down in your seat just in time for the meeting to begin.

It's not until about fifteen minutes into the service that you finally catch your breath and start noticing what's going on. Even then, your mind wanders, you wonder why Mrs. Smith in the choir chose to wear *that* dress today, and you struggle to stay awake during the sermon.

A profitable time of worship? Hardly. Glorifying to the one you are worshiping? Probably not.

It is unfortunate that many Christians really put very little thought into why they are gathering corporately, what they can do to prepare for corporate worship, and what they should be focusing on during the service. In this chapter, we're going to consider some biblical answers to these important questions.

The Purpose of Corporate Worship

Put very simply, corporate worship is Christians worshiping together with other Christians. If worship is essentially spiritual response to truth, then corporate worship is *corporate* spiritual response to truth.

Sunday morning should be time set apart by the local church for corporate worship. Yet not all Christians agree with that assertion. Some Christians question one or both of the claims of the statement, first that Christians must assemble on Sunday and second that they must assemble to worship.

The Day Belonging to the Lord

Christians should set apart every day unto to the Lord as a sacrifice of worship (Romans 12:1), but the first day of the week has been specifically distinguished from the other six days by God. This special day was prophesied in the Old Testament:

I thank you that you have answered me and have

become my salvation. ²²The stone that the builders rejected has become the cornerstone. ²³This is the LORD's doing; it is marvelous in our eyes. ²⁴This is the day that the LORD has made; let us rejoice and be glad in it (Psalm 118:21—24).

Christians often use this passage to teach that we should rejoice in every day that God has made. But more correctly this passage speaks of a specific day in which would should specially rejoice. This special day that the Lord has made is the one on which "the stone that the builders rejected has become the cornerstone." Peter explains what this special day is in Acts 4:10—11:

> Let it be known to all of you and to all the people of Israel that by the name of Jesus Christ of Nazareth, whom you crucified, whom God raised from the dead —by him this man is standing before you well. ¹¹This Jesus is the stone that was rejected by you, the builders, which has become the cornerstone.

Peter indicates that this special day prophesied in Psalm 118 is the day on which Jesus the Messiah raised from the dead, which all four Gospels tell us was the first day of the week.

This day of Christ's victory over sin and death is one in which Christians should rejoice in a special way different from the other six days of the week. This special set-apart day is specifically designated as "The Lord's Day":

I was in the Spirit on the Lord's day (Revelation 1:10).

This expression "Lord's Day" is not the same as other expressions in Revelation rendered "day of the Lord." The term translated "Lord's" in Revelation 1 is not the same term used in the other references. This is a unique term of possession indicating that because of Christ's resurrection, the first day of the week is a special day "belonging to the Lord."

While it is true that the expression "Lord's Day" is used only once in the New Testament, and it is not explicitly connected to the first day of the week, testimony of early church leaders, including some friends of the Apostle John, confirm that the first day was called "The Lord's Day." For example, Ignatius, a companion of John said, "Let us no more Sabbatize, but let us keep the Lord's day, on which our Life arose." Likewise Iranaeus, a disciple of Polycarp who was a friend of John said, "On the Lord's day every one of us Christians keep the Sabbath, meditating on the law, and rejoicing in the works of God." Since John's friends referred to the first day of the week as "The Lord's Day," there is no doubt to what John was referring in Revelation 1:10.

This same possessive term, "Lord's," is used in 1 Corinthians 11:20 with reference to the "Lord's supper." This biblical ordinance is a supper "belonging to the Lord" in a special way. It is a supper set apart from other common suppers because it symbolizes the death of Christ. Similarly, the first day of the week is set apart from other common days because it is the day on which Christ arose.

We find clear examples in the New Testament of churches gathering together on the first day of the week:

> On the first day of the week, when we were gathered together to break bread, Paul talked with them, intending to depart on the next day, and he prolonged his speech until midnight (Acts 20:7).

> On the first day of every week, each of you is to put something aside and store it up, as he may prosper, so that there will be no collecting when I come (1 Corinthians 16:2).

So well was the Christian observance of the Lord's Day known in the first centuries that pagan officials would ask, "Do you keep the Lord's day?" as equivalent to the question, "Are you a Christian?"

So it is clear that for a Christian, the first day of the week should be a special day set apart for God because it is a day especially belonging to him.

The Command to Worship Corporately

There are some who argue today, however, that when churches gather, their purpose is *not* for worship. Their purpose might be edification, evangelism, discipleship, and fellowship, but not worship. Essentially, people like this argue that worship should encompass all of life, not just Sunday morning. We worship every day of the week, they insist, and the gathering of the church is for other functions like fellowship and edification.

While it is certainly true that Christians should worship seven days a week and not just one, and while edification and fellowship are clearly part of the purpose of assemblies of believers, there is also clear indication in Scripture that God wants his people to worship corporately including in the local church.

In Psalm 149:1 we find a clear command to worship the Lord corporately: "Praise the LORD! Sing to the LORD a new song, his praise in the assembly of the godly!"

While it is certainly important to worship the Lord as individual believers, God evidently delights also in gathered worship. Yet there is no such explicit command in the New Testament. We do find commands to gather, such as in Hebrews 10:24—25, but no clear command to worship at such gatherings. The question becomes, then, whether the commands for Old Testament saints to worship corporately are sufficient as commands for New Testament saints.

The Examples of Corporate Worship

It is for this reason we turn to examples of what believers did as they obeyed the command to gather. In the Old Testament, one of the purposes for gathering was clearly worship:

> Praise the LORD! I will give thanks to the LORD with my whole heart, in the company of the upright, in the congregation (Psalm 111:1).

But is this also true of the New Testament? Let's examine an example of a church gathering. In fact, this example is of the very *first* church gathering. Certainly this gathering set precedent for those to come. We find such an example in Acts 2:42:

> And they devoted themselves to the apostles' teaching and the fellowship, to the breaking of bread and the prayers.

Luke lists four commitments to which these believers "devoted themselves" as they gathered for the first time as a church.

The first commitment of this infant church was devotion to apostolic teaching. They certainly had much to learn as new Christians, so the apostles instructed them in the teachings of Jesus, how he had fulfilled Old Testament prophesies, and how they should live with each other and be witnesses for Christ. And these people were devoted to this teaching as they gathered.

After a while, the apostles wrote down this teaching under the inspiration of the Holy Spirit. So now, we have this same apostolic teaching recorded for us completely in the letters of the New Testament. The apostolic teaching to which this infant church was devoted was basically the New Testament Scriptures that we have today.

This commitment illustrates the first important element of biblical worship — presentation of truth. Remember, worship cannot take place unless truth is presented, and so the fact that this first church gathering was devoted to truth is the first step towards worship.

Next, Luke says that they were devoted to "the fellowship." This word literally means "having in common." It is the same word used in verse 44 that is translated "had everything in common." What was it that these 3,000 new converts from all over the world had in common? Their new faith in Jesus Christ is what gave them unity.

This kind of unity is expressed throughout the New Testament with reference to the gathered church. This fellowship is not what we might normally call "fellowship" today — getting together for a piece of pie and talking about sports or politics. This kind of fellowship is gathering to enjoy what we "have in common," namely, our relationship with Jesus Christ. In other words, we are sharing with each other the responses of our spirits toward God. We are sharing in worship.

The third commitment was devotion to "the breaking of bread." There is a definite article in the text — "the" — which indicates that this is specifically speaking about the Lord's Table. This was something the first church was devoted to because Christ had commanded them to be devoted to observing the Lord's Table in the context of the gathered church.

What is significant about this ordinance of the church? In 1 Corinthians 11, Paul gives specific instructions to the church concerning participation in the Lord's Supper. But earlier in chapter 10 he explains the significance of the ordinance:

> [16]The cup of blessing that we bless, is it not a participation in the blood of Christ? The bread that

> we break, is it not a participation in the body of Christ? [17]Because there is one bread, we who are many are one body, for we all partake of the one bread.

The word translated "participation" here is the exact same word translated "fellowship" in Acts 2:42. It emphasizes what we have in common as the gathered church. It emphasizes the unity we share in Christ. It is often translated "communion," which is why we sometimes refer to the Lord's Table as "Communion."

The significance of this Communion is that we demonstrate together the unity and fellowship of worshiping Jesus Christ. This is why the ordinance was given to the church and not just individuals. This is why you can't just have a few friends to your home and have Communion — this is for the whole body to partake of together.

So this devotion to the Lord's Supper is another evidence of a unified expression of worship to the Lord. They committed themselves to this observance as a God-ordained means of expressing spiritual responses to God.

The fourth and final commitment Luke lists of this infant church is devotion to public prayer. Again, there is a definite article — "the" — in front of "prayers." It literally reads, "the breaking of bread and *the* prayers." This has two implications.

The first is that this is speaking about more than just individual, private prayer. Private prayer is important, but these believers were devoted to "*the* prayers," meaning public times of prayer together as a gathered church.

The other implication is that "the prayers" probably refers to specific prayers that were part of regular Jewish practice. It would have been quite natural for this exclusively Jewish Christian assembly to continue some of the worship practices they enjoyed in the Temple and synagogues, simply adding truth about Jesus Christ.

So these are the four devotions that occupied the attention of the first gathering of the church. Each of them describes elements of the biblical essence of worship — responding with our spirits to God's truth — only adding one more characteristic, that of communion with other believers in worship.

We see other examples of the gathered church participating in united worship as well. For example, later in Acts 2 Luke records that this same group was gathered, "praising God" (v. 47). Acts 13:2 likewise tells us that a gathering of Christians was "worshiping the Lord."

Therefore, we can see by example that the gathered church is simply participating in worship, but doing so in a united way.

Terms for Corporate Worship

While these commands and examples demonstrate that churches gather for the purpose of worship, probably the clearest evidence relates to the language used in the New Testament to describe what the church is and what it is supposed to do.

Consider, for example, Ephesians 2:19—22. I will cite the KJV translation of this particular passage because the Elizabethan pronouns of that language best reveal the underlying Greek plural designations. In other words, in King James English, "you" refers to a singular person and "ye" refers to a group.

> Now therefore **ye** are no more strangers and foreigners, but fellow citizens with the saints, and of the household of God; ²⁰And are built upon the foundation of the apostles and prophets, Jesus Christ himself being the chief corner stone; ²¹In whom all the building fitly framed together groweth unto an **holy temple** in the Lord: ²²In whom **ye** also are builded together for an **habitation** of God through the Spirit.

Paul is addressing the gathered church ("ye"), and he calls them a holy *temple* in the Lord. The word translated "temple" here is the same word used for the Holy Place in the Jewish Temple. If the church is described as the Holy

Place of the Temple, what do you think is supposed to occur when it gathers?

Likewise, In 1 Corinthians 3:9 the church is called God's "building" or "dwelling." In verses 16—17 of the same passage the church is once again called the Holy Place of God's Temple in which he "dwells." In 1 Peter 2:5 —9 the church is called the "spiritual house" of God in which we are to offer "spiritual sacrifices." The original Greek audience reading these texts would not have been able to help but notice the worship language used to describe what the church is and what it is supposed to do when gathered.

So among other purposes and functions of the church, it must set apart time for worship when it gathers. It must provide time for the presentation of truth about God and time to spiritually respond to that truth with one voice. This corporate worship should take place on that special day set apart from other days because of Christ's resurrection, the Lord's Day.

The Preparation for Corporate Worship

Recognizing that we gather on Sunday morning as a church with the purpose of worshiping our holy Lord should cause us to think seriously about how we are coming to worship. Remember, this is a day that belongs to the Lord in a special way just like the Lord's supper. We shouldn't approach the Lord's supper in a kind of unprepared, flippant manner that we would some other supper, and similarly, we must not approach the Lord's Day as we would just any other day. We find such an attitude in Ecclesiastes 5:1—2:

> Guard your steps when you go to the house of God. To draw near to listen is better than to offer the sacrifice of fools, for they do not know that they are doing evil. ²Be not rash with your mouth, nor let your heart be hasty to utter a word before God, for God is in heaven and you are on earth. Therefore let your words be few.

Here we find admonishment to "guard [our] steps," or "approach cautiously" when we come to corporate worship. This is not something to enter into lightly, rashly, or flippantly. Corporate worship is something for which we must prepare.

Unfortunately most people are not only *unprepared* for corporate worship when the Lord's Day arrives, they are *ill*-prepared. In other words, most people have set up their week, Saturday evening, and Sunday morning so that they *cannot* be adequately prepared.

Preparation Begins Monday Morning

Instead, we should begin our preparation for the next Lord's Day's corporate worship on *Monday morning!* This is accomplished mostly by how we plan our week. Plan your responsibilities so that you can have Saturday evening free. Plan your times of personal and family worship during the week to create anticipation for the corporate worship on the Lord's Day.

If your pastor is preaching through a particular book of the Bible on Sunday mornings, you will have a fairly accurate idea of the passage he will be preaching on the upcoming Lord's Day. Take time to read and meditate on that passage yourself and with your family during the week. If you're not sure what your pastor will be preaching, why not ask him ahead of time?

Likewise, ask your pastor what hymns will be sung on the next Lord's Day and use them in your times of personal and family worship. Teach the hymns to your children and help them understand what the hymn texts mean so that they can be prepared when the Lord's Day comes.

Preparation Intensifies Saturday Evening

Our preparation for corporate worship should intensify Saturday evening. For the most part it may be wise to leave Saturday evenings free from other activities. Plan your family times and gatherings with friends on Friday evening, not Saturday. Saturday evening should be given over to preparing for the Lord's Day.

We should be continuing our spiritual preparation on Saturday evening, perhaps having a special time of family worship, but we should also prepare practically. Saturday evening is the time for choosing clothes, finding shoes, bathing children, and packing the car, not Sunday morning. Giving careful thought on Saturday evening to what needs to be done will make the Lord's Day morning much less hectic.

Preparation Culminates Sunday Morning

If you have made sufficient preparation on Saturday evening, hopefully Sunday morning will be much more relaxed. But the preparation for corporate worship can still continue. Use your breakfast time or ride to the church building as a time to gather your thoughts and remember what you'll be hearing and singing in the morning service.

Plan to arrive at the church building with enough time for fellowship with your brothers and sisters in Christ, but with also enough time to find your seat and rest your mind in preparation for corporate worship. When you seat yourself prior to the service, commit to a time of prayer, reading of the Scriptures, or reviewing the upcoming service order so that you can be fully engaged once the service begins.

All of this preparation will certainly require planning and discipline, but if we see our corporate worship as something serious and important, we should be willing to put in the time and effort to prepare adequately for it. Remember, this is a special day belonging to the Lord, and for this reason we should look forward to it. The rewards of corporate worship will be far greater if we do.

The Participation in Corporate Worship

With all of this in mind, what should we be thinking as we worship on Sunday morning? Here are several suggestions.

Singing

Since every member of the congregation is responsible to participate in worship, then no element of the service is optional, including the singing. Just because you don't like to sing or don't think you have a good voice does not mean you can keep your mouth shut! Singing in church is not about the quality of your voice. Singing is about lifting our heart responses to the Lord. And by singing with others in the congregation, we are being helped to express right kinds of affections to God in worship and manifesting the unity of the body.

Offerings

Giving from money we have earned is one tangible way that we can express our hearts of thankfulness to the Lord and support for what he is doing through the church. We must also be aware of the congregational nature of our giving as well. We are not just giving as individuals, we are giving alongside our fellow Christians.

This is why I believe we should be prepared to give every time we worship corporately. Most of us have a particular percentage that we plan to give each time we earn money, and most people simply give that as an offering all at once. This means that depending upon when we get paid, we may only give once a month or once every two weeks.

But in order to demonstrate both the congregational nature of giving and the fact that we are thankful every time we gather for worship, perhaps a better practice would be to divide our planned giving so that we can give a portion every time we have a worship service.

Prayer

Like singing, every member of the congregation should be actively involved in corporate prayer. This means that when someone is leading in prayer, our minds should be actively engaged with him, affirming, "Amen" in our hearts many times during the prayer and certainly at the end of the prayer. In fact, it is a good practice for every member to verbally say, "Amen" at the end of a corporate prayer. This practice perfectly manifests the unified nature of corporate prayer.

Further, if someone needs to move to another location in the service, he should refrain from doing so during the corporate prayer. If you are scheduled to sing immediately following the prayer, for example, don't move into place during the prayer. How can you be actively engaged in the corporate activity if you are moving? Instead, move to your place before or after the prayer.

Special Music

I am not fond of the term, "special music," because it gives the impression that other music in the service, specifically the congregational singing, is not "special." Yet the times of congregational singing are actually the most important musical events of the service. Congregational singing is commanded in Scripture, and it demonstrates the unified nature of corporate worship. Even so, "special music" can sometimes be an aid to worship. Perhaps renaming it "prepared music" or "musical offering" would help.

But since these prepared musical offerings do not actively involve the entire congregation, sometimes church members can very easily slip into "spectator" mode or even let their minds wander. What can we do to prevent this from happening?

First, recognize that even during a vocal solo, choir anthem, or instrumental number, you should be actively participating. You are not a spectator watching a performance. You should be just as involved as those performing. These musical "leaders" are simply helping you have the right kinds of spirit responses and express them to God.

Second, there are things that you can do to help yourself participate. If an instrumental number is being performed, open the hymnal and consider the words of the song as an aid to keep your mind and heart active. Then ask, "What affections do this arrangement express that fit with the truths of this hymn?" If you don't know what hymn is being played or if you do not have access to the words, ask yourself what kinds of affections are being expressed through the music itself and what truths about God would solicit such responses.

With vocal music, listen to the musical arrangement and how the song is sung help to express different kinds of spiritual responses. Notice how those responses flow directly from the truth being sung.

Silence

If there is silent space between elements in the service, don't think, "Boy, I wonder who goofed" or allow the time to distract you. Instead, consider the truth and responses with which you just participated and anticipate what is to come. Perhaps use times of silence for prayer, thanking God for the things you just considered.

Preaching

The sermon is the most evident time in the service when truth about God is being presented. All through the sermon you should be considering the truths of the Bible and asking yourself how you should be responding. You may need to respond with confession. You may find yourself responding with joy and thankfulness.

No matter what *kind* of response you express, we

should always respond in some way to the preaching of God's Word. Sometimes we get the idea that we need to respond only when we are "convicted" or "spoken to." On the contrary, God's truth always demands a response, and remember that worship doesn't take place until we respond to truth.

Conclusion

In Hebrews 12:28–29 the author commands us to "offer to God acceptable worship, with reverence and awe, for our God is a consuming fire." This implies that there is such a thing as worship that is *not* acceptable to God.

It is very important for us, therefore, to consider carefully how we are worshiping. Do we prepare for it? Do we actively participate in it?

God deserves our worship, and he delights in the worship of his assembled people. Let's commit ourselves to worshiping deliberately, congregationally, intentionally, and actively.

Notes

1   Num. 21:17-18; Isa. 16:10; 27:2; Jer. 25:30; 48:33; Hos. 2:17; Zech. 4:7.
2   Num. 21:27-30; Ps. 68; 2 Chron. 20:21; Num. 10:35-36; Exod. 15:20; Judg. 5:1; 1 Sam. 21:12; Ps. 24:7-10.
3   Ps. 45; Song of Sol. 2:12; Ezek. 33:32; Isa. 5:1; Gen. 31:27; Jer. 25:10; 33:11; Isa. 23:15-16.
4   Job 21:12; Isa. 24:9; 2 Sam. 19:35; Lam. 5:14; Dan. 6:18; Amos 6:5.
5   Job 30:9; Lam. 3:14, 63; Isa. 14:4; 2 Sam. 1:18-27; 1 Kings 13:30; 2 Chron. 35:25; Ps. 69:12; Job 30:31; Eccles. 12:5; Jer. 9:16-17; 22:18; Ezek. 27:30-32.
6   *Homily on the First Psalm* 1 & 2, quoted from Strunk, *Source Readings in Music History* (New York: Norton, 1998), 11—12.
7   *Commentary on Psalm 1, 9*, quoted from McKinnon, *Music in Early Christian Literature* (Cambridge: Cambridge University, 1987), 126.
8   Quoted from Strunk, *Source Readings in Music History*, 14.
9   *In Psalmum XXXII Enarratio*, trans. in McKinnon, *Music in Early Christian Literature*, 356.
10 "Preface to the Burial Hymns" (1542), in Lehmann, *Luther's Works*, Vol 53 (Philadelphia: Fortress, 1965), 328.
11 "Preface," *Genevan Psalter*, 3.
12 Miscellany #188, *The "Miscellanies,"* 331.
13 I use the NASB translation of Colossians 3:16—17 here because I believe it better reflects the symmetry of the clauses than the ESV does. See David F. Detwiler, "Church Music and Colossians 3:16," *BibSac* 158: 631 (July 2001), 358.
14 Harold Best, *Music through the Eyes of Faith* (San Francisco: Harper, 1993), 52.
15 Ibid., 59.

CPSIA information can be obtained
at www.ICGtesting.com
Printed in the USA
FFOW04n0903151214
9516FF